T i✳

SCOTTISH
= MUSEUMS
COUNCIL

Her Majesty's Stationery Office
Edinburgh

The Scottish Museums Council is an independent company, funded primarily by the Scottish Education Department, whose purpose is to improve the quality of local museum and gallery provision in Scotland. This it endeavours to do by providing a wide range of advice, services and financial assistance to its membership.

Scottish Museums Council
County House
20-22 Torphichen Street
Edinburgh
EH3 8JB

© *Crown Copyright 1985*
First published 1985

ISBN 0 11 492430 9

Contents

Foreword

At a time when the whole system of museums in Scotland, national and local, is under consideration by important independent bodies, the theme "Museums are for People" is a pertinent reminder of the concern which should be central to both the profession's and the public's thinking.

Paradoxically, perhaps, a recurring theme of these essays is that museums need to become far more businesslike if they are to serve their public more effectively. Not so strange a thought, however, if we accept an encouragingly broad view of museums' functions: not only as educational and leisure facilities, but as creators of wealth and employment, generators of investment, attractors of tourists, and supporters of economic and cultural regeneration. In fact, if we simply accept them as an integral part of the service industry sector of our economy. As long as we remember all these aspects together, there is no cause to be ashamed of the practical and material side.

I should like to take this opportunity to thank all the contributors for sharing with us their insights and experiences and for undoubtedly sowing the seeds of many stimulating new initiatives in our museums.

Trevor Clark
Conference Chairman
Scottish Museums Council

The general public at the British Museum (Natural History).

Museums and their customers

Kenneth Hudson
Kenneth Hudson is the author of the UNESCO-sponsored *Museums for the 1980s* (1977), which was based on the worldwide research he undertook for the project. His other books include *A Social History of Museums* (1975) and two editions of *The Good Museums Guide*. With Ann Nicholls, he compiles every five years Macmillan's international *Directory of Museums*. He is at present working on *Museums of Influence,* to be published by the Cambridge University Press.

For the past eight years he has been the administrator of the European Museum of the Year Award and a member of the committee and jury of the British Museum of the Year Award.

The title of this paper could have been *Museums and the People who use them. Museums and their Public,* would have been inadequate, because I am not concerned only with the people usually classed as visitors. A museum is certainly a place to be visited, but it is also an important source of information, a place where enquiries can be dealt with in a reliable and authoritative way and where research can be carried on. Why then have I chosen to call my contribution *Museums and their Customers*?

I have done this deliberately, to emphasise my conviction that any museum, no matter what its size or character, is essentially a business. It receives and handles funds on behalf of the public. Members of the public are its customers and one of its prime duties is to do its best to meet their reasonable demands. It is not a good musem, however

splendid its collections and however admirable its conservation and display techniques may be, if it has too many dissatisfied customers. The museum's customer may not always be right, and he may on occasion be tedious, but he exists, he has a vote and he pays the taxes and the entrance fees which make it possible to continue.

I have no reason to claim to be a typical museum customer – such a person, fortunately, is a myth – but it is wiser to start with the known, rather than the unknown, so I begin with myself. I write about museums, I visit them professionally and for pleasure, I help to judge them for competition purposes, and I am constantly in need of the kind of information they possess. I am a many-sided customer, and I probably know more about museums and the way they function than is good for me. But, as a customer, I am concerned with getting value for money, and the purpose of this paper is to explain what I mean by value for money in museum terms.

First, may I say with all possible emphasis and clarity, that I am not in the least impressed by the big as such. One does not get better value from a museum merely because it is big. Precisely the opposite is all too frequently true. Hudson's First Law of Museums states that the speed and courtesy with which a member of the public obtains information from a museum is in inverse proportion to the size of a museum. One should perhaps add, in fairness, that museums are by no means unique in this respect. No matter what kind of organisation one has to deal with, larger nearly always means worse so far as relations with the public are concerned. I say "nearly always", because there are some most honourable exceptions among the big museums. I have always had splendidly prompt treatment from the Museum of London, the Victoria and Albert and the British Museum (Natural History), to take three examples which occur immediately to me. I would not dream of mentioning those prestigious museums from which I have had the most dilatory and disgraceful treatment, but anyone of a detective turn of mind can amuse himself with a little divination.

The fact that I myself am lucky or unlucky in digging out the information I need, information I know perfectly well the museum possesses, is only of fringe or perhaps symbolic significance. What is of far greater importance is that a little effort expended on collating the experiences of one's friends and acquaintances does certainly result in the sad conclusion that while many museums may talk bravely and boldly about "existing to serve the public", or some paraphrase of that, it does not seem to be well or widely understood that service consists of giving individual members of the public what they want – and giving it with a good grace – rather than handing out what is reckoned to be good for them.

What one is really criticising, of course, is a tradition and a system, rather than individuals. A large museum is essentially a special form of academic bureaucracy and, admirable and necessary people though they may be in other ways, neither academics nor bureaucrats are historically celebrated for their speed of action or for their tolerance and helpfulness to those outside the magic circle.

I remember having a conversation a few years ago with a systems analyst working for a large brewery group, Watneys. I asked him if he thought of himself as a computer-man who happened to be working for this particular brewing concern, or as a Watney-man who happened to be in charge of their computer section. Without a second's pause, he said he was a computer-man first and foremost and a Watney-man only very incidentally. I have often wondered what the answer would be if one put a similar question to a handful of museum directors. Did they regard themselves first as museum-people or first as scholars, civil servants or local authority employees? Pushed hard, where would they say their primary loyalty lay? With which breed did they identify themselves?

*Quarry Bank Mill, Styal.
An adult weaving class in
progress.*

*Quarry Bank Mill, Styal.
Part of the weaving room.*

The point is an important one, because, faced with this or that member of a museum's staff, the innocent outsider can so easily fall into the trap of confusing appearance and reality. He may not realise the extent to which an organisation can influence the behaviour and instincts of even the most kindly and well-meaning person. He may not recognise a local government employee when he sees one.

Government employees, whether local or national, work within a carefully constructed framework of rules and regulations. They protect themselves by being careful not to step a millimetre outside these regulations. They do what is contractually required of them and not a scrap more. If it is officially laid down that they will begin work at 9 a.m. and finish at 5 p.m., they will be deaf and invisible outside these hours. And, within the prescribed hours, their pace and intensity of work will be what they learnt from their elders and betters from the day of their arrival. What the public therefore gets is what fits the system. Man was made for the system, and not the system for man.

It is perfectly possible for a museum with a conventionally efficient, well-run public relations department to give a poor service to the public. The same is true, of course, of any other type of organisation – an industrial firm, a bank, British Telecom, a hotel chain – and the reason for the inadequacy is the concept of public relations as a one-way activity and its confusion with publicity. "Service", in museum terms, does not mean merely preparing exhibitions, running an education department, publishing booklets and postcards and all the other planned, controlled activities. It includes dealing promptly and reliably with questions, complaints and requests for facilities from the public, with matters which are unplanned, uncontrolled, and quite possibly inconvenient.

At this juncture, I feel obliged to point out two things. The first is that, within any sizeable organisation, however decrepit, out-of-date and dinosaur-like it may be, there is nearly always some devoted, unlikely, heretical throwback of a person who keeps the creaking machine working and stops it from seizing up completely. We have all come across such people. They are God-given and we are exceedingly grateful for their miraculous existence. And the second point is that in Britain, but not in France, the Netherlands and most other countries of the world, we have not one system of museums, but two, a public and a private. The size of the private system will probably come as a surprise to many people, even those who consider themselves well-informed about museums. The Association of Independent Museums calculates – on the basis of its membership list, which does not represent a closed shop – that there are about 600 museums in England, Scotland, Wales and Northern Ireland which are not run by the State or by a local authority. Some are private in the strict sense of the word, but most belong to a registered charitable trust. What they all have in common is that they depend for survival, to say nothing of growth and prosperity, on what the public pays in the form of entrance fees and of purchases in the museum shop and cafeteria. The salaries and wages and indeed the very existence of the museum depends on attracting and pleasing the public.

A visiting researcher studying rats at the British Museum (Natural History), London. A hundred such visitors are to be found at the Museum on any one day.

This is not the case with a local authority or a State museum. If the annual number of visitors to, say, the British Museum or Scunthorpe Museum were to be halved, it is extremely unlikely that any member of the staff of either museum would be declared redundant, and even more unlikely that the museum itself would shut down. In these circumstances, it would be surprising if "service" did not mean something rather different in the two sectors of the museum world, the public and the private. In the private sector, visitors have to be wooed, cosseted and pleased all the time. One's daily bread depends on it. In the public sector, it is nice if a museum or an exhibition is well-patronised, but it is not disastrous if it is not. I am sure this is the main reason why the queries I post and telephone to private sector museums

receive, on the whole, more satisfactory treatment than the ones which find their way to the public sector.

But, as I have already said, I am not necessarily a typical customer. My requirements may be peculiar, although not, I think, all that peculiar. What then is a fair method of assessing a museum's merits, its ability to satisfy its customers? How should the mark sheet be arranged?

There are, of course, those who would say this is not the proper approach. One should first ask the museum what it is trying to do and then discover how well or badly this aim is being fulfilled. I have tried this method and found it unsatisfactory, largely because most museums apparently find it very difficult to say what they are trying to do. Some get remarkably close to saying, "We're here because we're here", although they usually avoid such unsophisticated language. But some measure, some basis of judgment there must be, if one is to be in a position to criticise a museum in a constructive way.

What I am sure museums badly need is some form of consumer movement, which would continuously weigh one museum against another, much as *The Good Food Guide* has done for restaurants. Neither can expect to be universally welcomed by those at the supplying end of the industry. Museum people – that is, people who make their living from museums – are likely to say that only those within the profession are qualified to judge the quality of a museum, and precisely the same comment is heard from restaurant people – that outsiders lack the necessary understanding of the problems. It would take a supremely

A member of the academic bureaucracy at the British Museum (Natural History). One of five similar floors of fossil collections at the Museum.

honest person of either kind, of course, to say that the museum existed primarily, or at all, to provide the staff with as good a living and as pleasant a life as possible. Such an admission might be politically unwise, but it would be in no way dishonourable.

It is curious that no-one within the respective callings seems to demand that only actors or theatre managers are fit to assess plays or that only conductors or impresarios can be trusted to write newspaper articles about concerts. Music, the theatre, films, the ballet or painting, and television all have learnt to assume their professional critics, giving the public their views on what is good and less good, bad and less bad, horrible and sublime. Quite

why museums should claim immunity from what would seem a perfectly natural and desirable system is difficult to say.

Some years ago, in a mood of great daring, I decided to experiment with a book I called *The Good Museums Guide.* Considerable organisation was required. I persuaded a panel of 250 people, widely distributed over the British Isles, to report on the 1600-odd museums within this area. Wherever possible, they confined their attentions to museums within 20 miles of their home. They used a standard reporting form and they were instructed to write down their comments without fear or favour. The 400 museums which achieved the highest scores received an entry in the *Guide,* with a brief description of the contents of the museum, details of opening times and quotations from the reporting forms. There were symbols to indicate the museum's amenities. The quotations varied from "well-polished floors and door-handles", to "a perfect stopping-place on a busy holiday-route", and from "teas and scones are good value" to "plenty of life and colour and the objects make sense without any need for a lot of labels". The occasional unfavourable remark about a generally good museum was included – "Children would rapidly become bored"; "the lavatories are totally inadequate for a museum of this size and importance", and "the commentary machines no longer function".

At the end of the book, there was a short section called "Why they didn't make it". This consisted of quotations from reports on museums which had not been well thought of by members of our visiting panel.

There were comments on the building, the amenities and the housekeeping – "Extremely cold. This curtailed the reporter's visit" (South East); "Only the nimble can negotiate the genuine antique staircases" (East Anglia); "Empty frames left around in the galleries" (Wales).

The section headed *General Impression* produced some damning judgments – "This museum ought to be in a museum" (North East) – Dylan Thomas had once used precisely the same words about the museum in his home town of Swansea; "Horrible, ranks with the average French provincial museum" (South East); "Educational, but so uninspiring" (East Midlands).

Display, presentation, interpretation attracted very heavy fire – "Pillow-lace bobbins sharing a case with Neolithic axes" (South East); "Showcases with labels for non-existent objects" (Channel Islands); "Highly marred by Woolworth's lampshades" (South East).

And the staffing was often not all it should have been – "Suffered from a clapped-out curator. The sooner this museum is closed down the better" (South West); "The man at the counter appeared shell-shocked by school parties" (South East); "The person in charge belonged to the Parks Department" (Wales); "I was distracted by the playing of the caretaker's radio" (South West).

But, once again comes the accusation that one is not being "scientific". The sample is too small, it represents a very haphazard cross-section of people, and so on. This does not worry me. I am not, thank God, in the market research business, where the individuality has to be squeezed out of one's informants in order to make their opinions classifiable and computable. I do not know if my 250 informants are typical. What I do know is that they have interesting things to say and that through them the voice of the museum customer rings out loud and clear, in a way that it has not done previously. In any case, no matter how many reporters or interviewees one chooses, there can never be agreement as to who is to be considered a typical museum customer. I recall the words of Brian Morris at the International Council of Museums Conference in London in 1983 – "To ask 'who are the users of museums?' is to make a pointless enquiry. We all know who they are. They are scholars, connoisseurs, laymen with a specialist interest, school parties, families, curious children, old men who find it warmer inside than out; the whole of human life is there. And they will differ from time to time and from place to place. They are the public, the people".

When he said this, I think it was the free, public museum which Professor Morris had in mind. "Curious children" do not drift in and out of independent museums, where they have to pay to get in, and old men are not found dozing there, for the same reason. The customers of the independent museum tend to be a more purposeful lot, determined to get value for their money. I once asked Neil Cossons, in the halcyon days when he was running Ironbridge Gorge Museum, whom he considered to be his typical customers. Without a second's hesitation, he said, "a family of four and they've driven 35 miles to get here. The father's 34 and works in computers, the mother's 33 and a physiotherapist. There's a girl of ten and a boy of eight". It sounded convincing and good, and no doubt there was more than a germ of truth in it, but an hour at Ironbridge would certainly reveal a lot of people outside the stereotype. And tucked away in the background are always the researchers, who come to Ironbridge to beaver away in the archives at theses and look for illustrations for their books and articles. They're equally customers and Ironbridge does very well for them and by them. It's a good business.

To return to *The Good Museums Guide* for a moment. It's had two editions and, if I can find the strength, there may be a third and even a fourth. It pleased a lot of people and annoyed almost as many, especially those who ran museums that didn't get a place in the *Guide,* and the old-timers who objected to the criteria and found the whole idea of sifting and grading museums obscene and socially dangerous. But I think it had a certain shock value and encouraged people to think a little harder about what makes a museum good or bad, which was certainly the intention.

The method of considering every museum as a package of professional and public qualities is, in any case, capable of being usefully applied outside the pages of *The Good Museums Guide.* It is, in fact, the basis of the judging which goes on for the European Museum of the Year Award and for the Museum of the Year Award in Britain, where the judges take a close and careful look, not only at the collections and at the manner in which they are looked after and presented, but at such matters as managerial efficiency, staff relationships, the museum shop and cafeteria, attitudes towards visits, educational programmes, housekeeping and seats for resting tired feet. All these things, and a number of others, form part of the museum package and, as I have said earlier, big by no means always or usually means best, as experienced shoppers and eaters-out know very well.

It is foolish and self-defeating to adopt the trade union view and to attempt to make the outside world believe that all museums are equally good and that all members of museum staffs are paragons. Would only that it were so. In a real world, however, one needs to distinguish the excellent from the mediocre, the interesting from the dull, and the business of critics and consumer movements is to assist the process of discrimination. It is as well, too, to be able to recognise the centres of progress and experiment early on, at a time when they need encouragement most.

Pendulums swing, and there seems to be little doubt at the moment that the museum pendulum is swinging fairly fast and hard in the direction of entrepreneurial methods, entrance fees, value for money, maximisation of visitor-numbers and all the rest of the new market-place approach. This will undoubtedly do a lot of good and the customers will benefit in many ways. But there is a lot of resilience not to say inertia, in the system, and what one might call the New Museum Movement is not going to sweep away or brisk up all the dull, neglected museums and all the idle people who work in them. Ten years from now job demarcation lines, precedents and regulations will still be with us and directors will still be refusing to meet people after five or on Saturday mornings. Such blocks to progress may possibly be less marked, but they will continue to exist. The long-suffering consumer is not going to enter Paradise in a hurry.

But it is well to remember that inertia and resistance to change has its good side. Not all museums are suited to the high-yield approach and some are likely to suffer badly if they are forcibly subjected to it. I can think without difficulty of half-a-dozen well run, modest sized museums, where any attempt to double and treble the number of visitors and create an atmosphere of feverish activity would be disastrous. They are essentially quiet places and their usefulness to the consumer depends on that quality being maintained. I remember Stonehenge in its quiet days and big-business Stonehenge appals me. God preserve Sutton Hoo from a similar fate. The museum equivalents to Stonehenge and Sutton Hoo are waiting anxiously in the wings.

Entrance Tickets:
*SS Gt. Britain, Bristol,
1984.*

*Old Sturbridge Village,
Boston (USA), 1982.*

Visitor expectations of museums

Victor T C Middleton

After a career in market research and marketing for commercial organisations and the British Tourist Authority, Victor Middleton is now:

Senior Lecturer (part-time) at the University of Surrey, responsible for marketing studies in the context of tourism.

Marketing Planning Consultant to the Wales Tourist Board.

Associate Consultant with Ventures Consultancy Ltd of Beaulieu – involved in work for local authorities, museums, historic houses and others concerned with visitor activities.

He is a Fellow and a Council member of the Tourism Society and has published many articles and lectured in many parts of the world in his subject area.

Underlying this paper are two central themes. The first is that visitor attitudes to and expectations of museums are currently in a state of transition. From a long tradition of relatively passive acceptance of whatever is provided (especially if it is free), museum visitors are increasingly revealing relatively active expectations and seeking nationally and internationally acceptable standards (especially if they pay). While any such transition takes many years to achieve its full impact, this change has been evolving for over a decade and it is related to increasing sophistication among museum visitors and to growing competition for attendances especially from private sector museums and other visitor attractions. The transition has to be seen also in the context of financial prospects for museums summarised recently by Sir Roy Strong as "Government is no longer able to fund our national collections on the scale needed to keep either their fabrics in repair or their displays up to date". This comment is of course equally applicable to most local authorities and boards of trustees responsible for regional and local collections. It focuses attention on the need to generate revenue from visitors, with or without admission charges.

The second theme is that museums are by definition locked into an unchanging world of clearly defined historic periods and

Hurdle making, Singleton Open Air Museum, Sussex, 1984.

Tinsmith at Old Sturbridge Village, Boston (USA), 1982.

largely fixed objects which encourage an understandable and in many ways proper preoccupation with collections and their intrinsic values. Psychologically, curators are inclined to look inwards to their collection and conservation needs, rather than outwards to potential visitors and their needs for information, display, entertainment and education. Such inward looking preoccupations have evidently dominated the museum world while outside it there has been what amounts to a revolution in customer expectations as well as massive change in the opportunities available for the public.

It is the juxtaposition of changing demand patterns and a relatively unchanging museums approach which now creates a management problem of a very complex nature. Responding to demand and developing a market orientated approach will not come easily to many museums. Mistakes will occur, formulas will be advanced and followed to the detriment of some museums, and damage leading in some cases to insolvency may well follow from crude attempts at market orientation. There are no simple recipes for quick success. But neither is there much prospect of standing still without attempting change. It is however certain that a better knowledge of consumer expectations is a vital first step in responding to a changing environment.

The discussion in this paper is in three parts. The first part considers the sort of people who are visitors to museums; the second part identifies ten visitor expectations; the third part draws some brief conclusions which are relevant to a management response.

So far as possible, the judgments expressed are based on recent research in which the author has been involved and on reports of other research carried out for museums. (The sources are noted at the end of this paper.)

The focus is on the broad majority of visitors who constitute the bulk (over 80 per cent) of most museum attendances. The paper does not deal with minority groups because of space constraints but in no sense is the value and importance of such groups underestimated.

In overall terms it is very clear that museums at national and local level draw the bulk of their customers from the more affluent sectors of the British population. Compared with the national average of 24 per cent of all British adults who visited a museum in 1981, 41 per cent of the top socio-economic group visited compared with only 14 per cent of the lowest group. Predictably, museum visiting is associated with higher levels of education, with people completing education at age 15 comprising less than one in five of all visitors in 1982. Less predictably, the over 55 age group appears much less likely to visit the museums than the under 45s, accounting for only about one in ten of all museum visitors (national and local). Many of the younger visitors will have experienced museum visits through the organised school parties which have become so vital a component of most museum attendances.

Most importantly, it appears that museum visitors have considerable experience of what is available in the museum world with two out of three making repeat visits to the same museum and making between four and five visits a year (1981) to other museums.

Thus in general terms, visitors to museums are drawn from that section of the population which is more than averagely articulate about its needs and expectations, more than averagely aware of choices open to it, more than averagely experienced in travelling around Britain and overseas and more than averagely capable of assessing the worth of local museums against other attractions and in terms of developed standards. They are in other words much more sophisticated as customers than was true a decade ago and the process is unlikely to reverse. They are also virtually universally exposed to high quality colour television bringing images and spectacular displays of the highest international standards into their homes.

Of the range of consumer needs and expectations, the following ten are selected as being broadly applicable to most museums. It is decisions on how best to respond to these needs in local circumstances which will determine future levels of visitor attendances and expenditure.

Visitors expect:
1. Value for money and effort.
   Even where an admission price is not payable, the effort for most people in arranging a museum visit should not be underestimated. In almost every case it involves allocating time, arranging transport, walking and standing and mental activity – in competition with alternative activities and attractions. The visit decision is based upon an assumption that the effort will be worth while. If it is not, or barely so, the prospect of repeat visits is low and of unfavourable word of mouth comment, high.

2. To plan a visit.
   Associated with the previous point, the evidence strongly suggests that the number of people who stumble upon museums while passing the doors is a tiny minority of all visitors. The great majority plan in advance and select a museum as the object of their outing.

3. To find a visit rewarding.
   Having made a decision to visit, museum visitors are looking for stimulation, entertainment and, to some extent, an opportunity to learn. They also seek novelty in the form of new exhibits or new displays. Visitor response to the events and special exhibitions staged at some museums is one indication of this search for variety. Reflecting their growing sophistication, visitors are also expecting to be involved in some way, physically through the senses, emotionally in the reaction of surprise, or shock, horror, pathos or pleasure, or mentally in the effort which has to be made to understand displays.

Without abandoning the objects of scholarship or sacrificing the integrity of collections to crude commercial exploitation, the way in which a museum provides a rewarding visit is a function of creative interpretation. The scope for such interpretation, employing modern technology as necessary, provides a challenge for every museum.

Catering standards:
Portsmouth Historic Naval Base, 1984

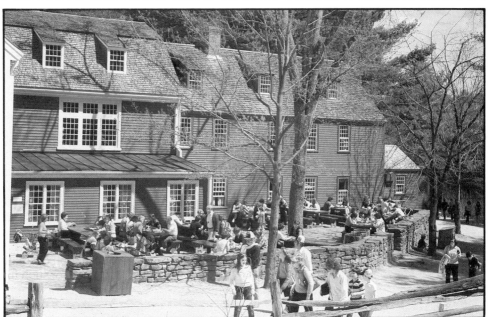

Old Sturbridge Village, Boston (USA), 1982.

Information Centre,
Beaulieu, Hants, 1982.

4. Not to know much about the collection.
   All museums have their specialist
   customers who study and research the
   collections and archive material. In
   almost every case they are a tiny
   minority. The bulk of visitors have very
   little prior knowledge and must either
   absorb it very rapidly from the nature of
   displays and the quality of information
   provided, or go away with very little
   appreciation of the interest and value
   inherent in the collections they have
   walked past.

5. To be guided.
   Following from the fourth point, most
   visitors will not know how to use their
   time to best advantage, how to
   understand the logic (if there is one) of
   the layout of exhibits and rooms, which
   route to follow when there are several
   floors or more than one building, which
   is best for children and so on. Most will
   not buy a guide book (or remember to
   bring the one they bought previously).
   Most will be diffident about
   approaching museum staff and will not
   ask them questions which might display
   ignorance. The function of guiding
   people and circulation flows around
   museums is a subject for careful
   consideration and experimentation.
   Successful guiding must be a highly
   relevant input to a rewarding visit.

Willing to queue:
*Mary Rose Ship Hall,
Portsmouth, 1984.*

6. To find high standards of service.
Related to the aspect of guiding is the general standard of services expected. This includes toilet facilities, cafeteria, shops, attendant courtesy and helpfulness (when approached), seats at strategic points. Where admission is charged the quality of reception at the admission point is a vital part of this expectation.

7. Not to stay long, but to queue if necessary.
Demonstrating point 4, it is remarkable how short a time people spend in museums. Less than one hour in most local authority museums and, even for overseas visitors on holiday, the British Museum keeps half its visitors for under two hours. This short duration is a vital element in planning circulation routes and location of key displays. It is also relevant to creating desires for repeat visits. The willingness to queue is not just a British phenomenon and appears quite acceptable if the end result is rewarding. It is possible that a queue signals something worth seeing and becomes an informal aspect of the guiding expectation noted above, in some cases no doubt, *faute de mieux*.

8. To pay, if they have to.
The evidence is clear that the majority of

people are willing to pay if they have to, but the implementation of charging which is not backed up by the satisfaction of visitor expectations and in relation to perceived value for money is a certain recipe for loss of visitors. Charging must be seen not as an absolute factor but as a function of length of stay which in turn is related to satisfaction achieved and visitor perceptions of value for money. All three factors are readily measurable.

9. To have opportunities to spend money.
    Whether or not they pay for admission (and the two aspects are not inversely related) visitors do patronise shops and many are willing to pay large sums for high quality gifts and souvenirs. The number of purchases and expenditure per head is related to the siting of shops, the range and attractiveness of displays and the quality of service provided. Poor quality goods in badly sited shops are unlikely to command attention and here at least (as distinct from inside the museum itself) queuing is not acceptable.

10. To go away satisfied.
    The tenth point repeats the first and is implicit in other points. It is impossible to over-emphasise the need to send away satisfied customers. Maintaining and improving on levels of satisfaction is the only certain way of knowing whether or not museum management policies and standards of service are keeping up with or improving upon competitive alternatives in the rapidly changing sphere of visitor expectations.

Some museums may find daunting this list of expectations and the implications for museum management. It is more daunting perhaps to consider that some museums and many visitor attractions are already responding to consumer needs with an obvious danger that others who do not will be left behind.

Three points are worth stressing. Firstly, visitor expectations can be determined and assessed in aggregate terms but they have to be measured in specific terms at each museum if the correct response is to be made. There is ample evidence to show that visitors can readily discriminate between museums on key aspects requiring management attention such as sign-posting, quality of displays, friendliness of staff and value for money. But these factors cannot be guessed at by curators, they have to be measured and monitored over time.

The second point is that museums have marvellous opportunities arising from the nature of their operations to experiment and monitor visitor reactions. Reaction to new displays, new circulation patterns, sales revenue at re-arranged shops or through changing menu items and catering style, visitor response to different types of events – the list of experimentation is almost limitless. To be of value to museum managers, however, experiments must be planned in relation to specific objectives and the results systematically monitored and analysed.

The third point is that visitor expectations tend to be inextricably interlinked and not compartmentalised as shown for the purposes of this paper. It is not an option to solve one expectation (such as queuing) and ignore the others. An effective management response must be relevant to the whole of the visitor's experience.

Looking ahead over the next two decades, the need to satisfy customer expectations and operate museums in a businesslike way appear likely to dominate the thinking of most museum curators and managers. Success is certain to be achieved in a competitive environment which reflects visitors' choices. "Paralysis by analysis" is a not uncommon jibe aimed at people who advocate research-based methods for management operations. It has an element of truth in it. The greater truth perhaps lies with an alternative management style "extinct by instinct". For curators, of all people with a lively sense of history, this latter danger is surely not without ample precedents.

Sources

1. Sir Roy Strong, *The Financial Times,* 26 April, 1984.
2. University of Surrey, *Survey of Overseas Visitors to Museums in London,* British Tourist Authority, 1983.
3. *Museums and Art Galleries as an Attraction for Overseas Visitors,* British Tourist Authority, 1982.
4. *Visitors to Museums Survey,* 1982, English Tourist Board, 1982.
5. "Open Sesame," a comment by Sir Arthur Drew, in *Tourism in England No 41,* Summer 1982, English Tourist Board.
6. *Museums – Lessons from the USA,* British Tourist Authority, 1983.
7. Kenneth Hudson, "Britain's Services Museums" in *Illustrated London News,* October, 1983.
8. Neil Cossons, "The New Museum Movement in the UK", 1983, *Museums Journal.*
9. *Interpretative Techniques at Historic Buildings,* English Tourist Board, 1982.
10. *Interpretation in Visitor Centres,* Dartington Amenity Research Trust, 1979.

Cultra Manor: Centrally sited in the Ulster Folk and Transport Museum's 176 acre estate, the Manor was formerly the Museum's administrative headquarters but has since become the centre of its education department.

The social significance of folk museums

George Thompson

George B Thompson was appointed in 1959 to be the first Director of the Ulster Folk and Transport Museum.

A graduate of The Queen's University of Belfast, he entered the museum profession in 1949 as Keeper of the Departments of Antiquities and Ethnography in the Belfast Museum and Art Gallery (now the Ulster Museum). He was a Fulbright Scholar (USA 1953), a foundation member of the Committee on Ulster Folklife and Traditions (now The Ulster Folklife Society), and also of the Society for Folklife Studies. He is a member of the Editorial Board of Ethnologia Europaea and a committee member of the Association of European Open Air Museums.

His service on public boards and councils includes the Historical Monuments Council (Northern Ireland), The Arts Council of Northern Ireland and the Northern Ireland Tourist Board. He was awarded an OBE in 1977 for services to museum development in Northern Ireland.

While the fact that all of my 35 years to date in the museum profession have related to the development of a folk museum may enable me to some extent to consider, and comment on, the subject assigned to me, I must admit that in approaching the task I am more conscious of my limitations than my qualifications. The social significance of folk museums is a big subject and to treat it comprehensively would not only require more space than has been allotted to me, but would call for considerably more knowledge and experience than I possess.

My entry into museum work in 1949, more or less directly from university, was determined more by fate than ambition. Ambition came later, but not before another stroke of fate provided me in due course with the rare privilege of becoming the first director of a new state folk museum initiated in Northern Ireland by Act of Parliament in 1958. In the preceding years, while working in a more conventional, multi-disciplinary museum, I had been involved in the promotion of the proposal that a folk museum be established

27

in Northern Ireland. For me these were the formative years when the fledgling graduate's naive idealism and resultant urge to become actively involved in social "do-goodery" came face to face with reality. My greatest disillusionment related to the social function of the museum, where I soon began to feel that the gap between the ideal and the actual was immense; that museum service to the public, relative to its possibilities, was more lip service than real service. It was this more than anything else that led me to favour the folk museum over the multi-discipline type of institution and brought me to a critical point early in my career when I had to choose between leaving the profession or staying on in the hope that the proposed folk museum would materialise in time and perhaps offer me an opening.

So, in the formative years, I began to develop a rationale which, from time to time, and in response to new experience and changing circumstances, has been added to and adjusted, and whose influence is reflected, for better or worse, in the policy and activities of the Ulster Folk Museum.

I propose, therefore, to draw upon it, and if it relates more to a specific folk museum than to folk museums in general, I hope that it yields some thought and opinions of general relevance.

Folk museums, by illustrating the day-to-day history of man within the country or region in which they function, confine themselves to a responsibility which is undeniably theirs. In comparison, many older, more conventional museums and their direct descendants which, especially

in Europe, often originated as private collections before becoming public institutions, represented an attitude towards the study of man which was, to a large extent, non-domestic and often world-wide in its embrace. In contrast to this their attitude to the public they purported to serve could be as restricted as their collecting policy was unlimited. In his book "A Social History of Museums", Kenneth Hudson comments, with respect to the British Museum – a public institution since the mid-18th century – that its "original rules and regulations . . . seem to have been expressly calculated to keep the public out and to make sure that the few who eventually did make the tour (one was not free to wander at will) got as little profit from it as possible"[1].

This elitist, 18th century definition of "public" could be seen as having an affinity with the view that man the anthropologist and anthropological man were not one and the same – that the latter was distinguishable by at least three characteristics; he was inferior, foreign, and any colour but white! Thus, man the anthropologist not only was possessed of an urge to study anthropological man, but also claimed the right to dispossess him of his artefacts, and if from the British Isles, he had a vast empire in which to operate, the pickings were rich and varied. This trend spread in time to the New World: the United States of America, a younger nation lacking the opportunities of imperial power, applied instead the power of financial wealth to acquiring for its museums vast collections from worldwide sources. Today, a changing outlook has led to museums holding such resources being faced with a growing demand from nations – often former

Kilmore Parish Church.

Kilmore Parish Church interior.

Coskib hill farm.

colonies but now independent states – for the return of cultural property: one might say that the anthropological specimen of the imperialist is coming to be regarded as the folk artefact of the new nationalist.

This is essentially a moral problem both complex and difficult and personally I am happy to leave those directly involved to wrestle with it, for in my view it is a problem with which folk museums are not concerned. In contrast to museums of the more conventional kind, the folk museum was conceived and established as a public institution responding to a public need. Let me again quote Kenneth Hudson, who, in his admirable book "Museums for the 1980s" reports that "At the 10th General Conference of the International Council of Museums held in Copenhagen in 1974, it was made clear that museums throughout the world are coming to regard themselves less and less as self-contained professional units and more and more as cultural centres for the communities within which they operate. One could summarise the change by saying that museums are no longer considered to be merely storehouses or agents for the preservation of a country's cultural and natural heritage, but powerful instruments of education in the broadest sense. What a museum is attempting to achieve has become more important than what it is".[2]

This description of a change in outlook by museums in general is, to my mind, a fair description of the outlook which the folk museum has had since birth. My scant knowledge of its origin, or rather the origin of the philosophy in which it was conceived, indicates that it stems from the

Kitchen of farmhouse from Corridreenan West.

great social upheaval generated at the end of the 18th century by revolutions in America and in France whereby the common man, so to speak, successfully challenged privileged power and began to take charge of his own destiny, but assumed thereby a responsibility which, educationally, he was ill equipped to bear.

Radical change, born of revolution and heightened by technical discoveries of immense potential, heralded a future which, dependent upon the beholder, could either be an exciting challenge full of great promise, or a source of fear and anxiety. In either event, the past assumed a new significance; it could be seen as a source of inspiration and learning, and a guide to the future, or it could be a means of escape from a future frightening to contemplate. Of the various titles suggested

as being applicable to the 19th century, one is "The Age of History" – the period in which evolved "a great idolatry of the past". And, in passing, one is tempted to suggest that a similar phenomenon is observable today in a social/technological revolution embodying the awesome potential of nuclear power, in the extent to which conservation of the past has for some become almost a religious crusade, augmented by a proliferation of history societies (in the past few years some 36 have emerged within Northern Ireland's small community) and collectors industriously assembling hordes of almost anything collectable.

The concept of romantic nationalism was also a product of 18th and 19th century change which gave significance to anything (arts, crafts, music, language,

*The Lismacloskey House:
an early 18th century
house with 19th century
extension, formerly located
near Toomebridge, Co.
Antrim, and transferred to
the open-air section of the
Ulster Folk and Transport
Museum in 1972/73. The
terrace houses being
reconstructed in the
background represent the
first phases of the
reconstruction of a small
Ulster town in contrast to
the dispersed rural
buildings featured
elsewhere in the open-air
museum.*

*Upper bedroom,
Lismacloskey House.*

dress, custom and belief) illustrative of national or regional identity, and made of them a source of enthusiastic study and inspiration for the thinkers and reformers of the day.

Here, then, were the elements which spawned new institutions concerned with the study and understanding of man, but in contrast to a situation where exalted man studied inferior man, the aim now was that man should study himself – a revival, you might say, of the simple and profound exhortation of classical philosophy – know thyself.

The folk museum was one of these institutions and in identifying it one tends also to think of the folk high school conceived by the Danish cleric and educationalist, Nicolai Grundtvig. As you may know, the first folk museum owes its conception and establishment to the Swede, Artur Hazelius, also an educationalist. Nordiska Museet was founded by Hazelius in Stockholm in 1873, to be followed in 1891 by an outdoor complement which took the name Skansen from its locality.

The folk museum differed from more established museums in illustrating man at home as opposed to man abroad. It collected, conserved, studied and exhibited the artefacts and vernacular architecture representative and evocative of the region in which it was located. As seen by Hazelius, it aimed to be not only an exposition but an environment comprised of local cultural history which would bring people together in an atmosphere of shared tradition, thus encouraging them, through a new knowledge of their past, to sense a

new pride in their past and in themselves as its inheritors – a pride based on fact, not fancy; a pride conditioned by a humility of self-understanding as opposed to a pride inflated by ignorance and self delusion.

Most, if not all, of today's folk museums acknowledge Hazelius's prototype as their primary inspiration. My own institution is no exception despite its late emergence, and it is to it that I should like now to turn.

Considering the influence of nationalistic feeling in the promotion of folk museum development – the Welsh Folk Museum is a case in point – one would have expected the nationalistic southern Republic of Ireland, rather than the northern Province of Ulster to espouse the folk museum cause. But Ireland often prefers the paradox to the orthodox, and so, paradoxically, it has been in Ulster, where nationalism is at best a source of controversy and at worst a lethal ideology, that a folk museum has been established on an international scale. The catalyst in Ulster came, not from the community at large, but from the university and the development of geography as an established subject in its own right under the inspired leadership of a Welshman, Estyn Evans.

No one in recent times has done more than Evans to study the Irishman in Ireland, to survey the evolution of human settlement in Ireland throughout the whole span of human occupation, and to understand how the resultant personality of the country and its people stems from the interaction of man and his physical environment.

It is generally accepted that it was Evans who, in the 1930s, following a visit to

Scandinavia, first proposed that a folk museum be established in Ulster. The intervention of World War II followed by post-war circumstances often beyond the control of those, including myself, who had become recruited to the folk museum cause, meant that the establishment of the museum did not occur until 1958. But with the benefit of hindsight one can see that in a number of essential respects this was a blessing in disguise.

As I stated at the outset, the Ulster Folk Museum was formally brought into being by Act of Parliament passed by the Government of Northern Ireland in 1958, an event which, to the best of my knowledge, is unique in the century-old history of folk museums in general. Looking back from the tragic situation which characterises Ulster at the present time, it is sad to think that the Ulster Folk Museum was established in a climate of optimism rather than of foreboding. One recognised the new museum as being timely in that it had a capacity, if developed wisely and imaginatively, to contribute to, and assist, a growing liberalism in the Ulster community and a desire to break away from old and divisive tribal loyalties. But, as we are now painfully aware, events were to take a different turn, though so far as the museum's social significance is concerned, they merely underlined it and emphasised the urgency of translating theory into practice. In the Parliamentary Act which established it, the museum was briefed to "illustrate the way of life, past and present, and the traditions of the people of Northern Ireland." In other words, in relation to the people of Northern Ireland, the museum was briefed to promote self-knowledge, and to do so impartially and as comprehensively as possible. Consequently it had as much, if not more, relevance to the contemporary social scene as any of its counterparts elsewhere have had in the past, or may have in the present within their respective regions: nowhere is the need for self-knowledge and understanding more real or urgent than in the Ulster community, where life has become so conditioned by the adopted and divisive identities of religious adherence and political persuasion as to stifle the influence and inspiration of a cultural identity which is largely shared. In Ulster, as in Ireland generally, concepts of what history comprises, and the limits of how much of their history is known and understood by Irish people in general, are, to say the least, variable, despite a popular belief in the outside world that we share an Irish obsession with history – an inability to forget it. However, I incline to a different view – one which has been admirably expressed by the Ulster historian Dr. Tony Stewart that "... the Irish are not only capable of forgetting the past, but of quite deliberately expunging from their minds whole areas of it. Like other nations, they have woven for themselves a garment of myth and legend which they call Irish history. Having designed it themselves, they have taken great care to make it as comfortable as possible, eliminating the loose threads and sharp edges, and making it so snug and warm that when they are wearing it they sometimes imagine themselves to be immune to the ordinary dictates of humanity. To the Irish all history is applied history and the past is simply a quarry which provides ammunition to use against enemies in the present. They have little interest in it for its own sake. So, when it is said that the Irish are too much

Tullylish Bleach Green Watch Tower and Ballyduggan Weavers' House.

influenced by the past, what is meant is that they are too much influenced by Irish history, which is a different matter."[3]

This situation is compounded by the formal teaching of history, which, in academic contexts, tends towards constitutional and political issues. The French naturalist, Jean Henri Fabre summarised it neatly when he observed that history "celebrates the battlefields whereon we meet our death, but scorns to speak of the ploughed fields whereby we thrive; it knows the names of the King's bastards, but cannot tell us the origin of wheat."[4]

Here is a comment which we in Ireland could acknowledge as being all too applicable to ourselves, and the events of the past 15 years have added substantially to our stock of battle monuments and martyrs. But, figuratively speaking, the message of the ploughed field and the origin of wheat has yet to be heeded and it is in remedying this that a folk museum, if properly conceived and put to work, can play a significant part. It is this that the Ulster Folk Museum seeks to do. It is a task more easily expressed than executed. History of whatever kind is evidentially fragmented and is consequently all the more difficult to interpret and understand. Where the history of day-to-day life is concerned, we in Ireland have conceivably made the situation all the more difficult because of a cultural "chemistry" in which intransigence and a strong romantic streak have played a prominent part in influencing our interests and activities as a result of which we have squandered much of the innate abilities and inclinations by

Kitchen interior of a two-roomed, thatched vernacular house from the Sperrin Mountain area of Co. Tyrone. The house is of the byre-dwelling type comprising a kitchen, bedroom and cow-byre beneath the bedroom and was re-erected in the Ulster Folk and Transport Museum in 1975/76.

which basic identity is normally translated into familiar and distinctive popular form. Comparing our culture with others elsewhere, no more generously endowed by nature than ours, and often less so, one could ask of Ireland some pertinent questions. Where, for example, is there a richness of visual folk art? Where is there a popular symbolism that is not coloured Republican green or Unionist orange? Why in the folk music repertoire do songs of rebellion dominate over songs of love, often in performance afloat on a sea of alcohol? Where in the more developed field of literary endeavour is there a substantial body of output divorced in theme from protest or self-justification or a renascent Celticism of doubtful validity? Where in

the composition of music evocative of spirit and identity is our Sibelius, Grieg or Dvorak?

I exaggerate, of course. Perhaps, too, I reveal a trace of cynicism for it is hard to resist in the light of current events. But I contend that the principle of my argument still holds good and that we in Ireland have a cultural problem that is both fundamental and immediate. However, identifying it is one thing; resolving it is quite another.

I have already indicated that so far as Ulster is concerned we see this problem as providing the Ulster Folk Museum with its principal objective. The means whereby it seeks to pursue and achieve that objective is seen as being located essentially in education – the identification and fulfilment of an educational function in the context of general education provision within the Province. All other museum activity – research, technical and curatorial – is for purposes of equipping the institution to act as effectively as possible as an educational medium.

As yet the museum is far from being completely built and staffed and so the extent to which we have been able to put principle into practice has, so far, been limited. Nevertheless, in testing the soundness of our ideas we have met success disproportionate to the modesty of our present provision. We have proved to our satisfaction that in developing the museum's educational possibilities there is great scope for innovation inspired by the circumstances which prevail in the community at large. But I should like to refer particularly to an attempt we made in the early 1970s to test our educational wings. We were motivated by the fact that civil unrest had given way to widespread violence involving in particular the younger generation. Amongst the measures introduced by government in an attempt to penetrate the root causes of the trouble was the establishment of a Ministry of Community Relations embodying a Schools' Community Relations Project. With the co-operation and assistance of the latter, the museum arranged for a group of 40 young people, half of them Protestant, half Roman Catholic, from the upper forms of secondary schools, to come to the museum for a week to undergo a course on local folk tradition with the emphasis on common heritage. These were young people of average academic ability, nearing the end of their secondary education and so on the threshold of full adult status and responsibility.

In a concentrated week's course at the museum we sought to provide them with an insight into the social/cultural past of which they were the descendants and the inheritors. To most, if not all, Ulster culture was coloured Republican green or Unionist orange. With us they found a culture that was not so polarised, but was discernible in softer and less emotive colours: it was the blue of the flax blossom, white as bleached linen, yellow as freshly churned butter, brown as turf, red as the heart of the blacksmith's forge. It was, too, a culture of sound; the clatter of the shuttle on the handloom, the lilt and cadence of vernacular speech, the song sung in the kitchen ceilidh. It could also be smelled as the sweet scent of home-baked bread or the pungent reek of turf smoke. It was the history of the ploughed field, not the battlefield.

The response of our young particpants by way of interest and understanding exceeded all our expectations. They saw, as we hoped they would, but feared that they might not, a past which they shared in common, and, with those distant horizons which only youth can anticipate, they recognised themselves as embodying the future of their common past.

Since then, the museum has ventured, albeit tentatively, into other areas of educational activity, for its capacity to teach and influence is not confined to the younger generation. The adult may be somewhat beyond the formative years, but he bears the heavy responsibility of

Agricultural Gallery (1981): One of three formal display areas within the Ulster Folk and Transport Museum's first custom-built exhibition gallery. Development plans include the addition of further galleries wherein systematic displays will complement the naturalistic presentation of folklife in the open-air section of the Museum.

trusteeship over the inheritance of his offspring, and he has the power to enhance or despoil that inheritance. It is my view, and that of my colleagues, that there is no field of adult endeavour concerned with the development and well-being of our community which could not benefit from a fuller knowledge and understanding of its folklife. Planners, designers, teachers, administrators, industrialists, communicators, politicians, could, with advantage, supplement whatever knowledge and criteria direct their activities, by some study and appreciation of the historical origins and character of the habitat and society in which they operate.

My thesis is a simple one. I hope it is also a worthy one. Perhaps its worthiness, if any, derives from its simplicity. The past and the future are not dissociated. Though of indefinite extent, they are, nonetheless, the extremities of a continuum. What the latter may hold for us and our succcessors, will reflect whether or not we consult or ignore the former. The philosopher Bertrand Russell observed that one of the great faults of our 20th century was that it limited itself by its "parochialism in time." Yet we inhabit an age in which we can least afford to be parochial in relation either to time or space. The distance separating man's baser instincts from the intelligence and perspective needed for the wise and constructive control of modern technical capability is frighteningly wide. We in Ulster, for example, need look no farther than our own doorstep to see how base instinct can dominate over intelligence and that where the lessons of the past are concerned we suffer from mass myopia.

To conclude, let me return briefly from an Ulster situation to a more general one.

Seven years ago, at the Museums' Association Annual Conference in Bradford I contributed a short paper[5] to a session concerning "The Museum's Role in a Changing Society." I ended it with some observations which, seven years on, are, I feel, still relevant, and I leave it to you to relate them to recent events both at home and abroad.

Speaking then about an Ulster situation, I suggested that it was peculiar to Ulster only in matters of detail, but that in general terms it illustrated a state of affairs that could happen anywhere and that signs of this were clearly in evidence. Irish Republicanism versus Ulster Unionism, or Catholic versus Protestant, are only local versions of a phenomenon that is world-wide. Race, colour, political ideologies, class distinction, economic imbalance, can all generate social change, even more so can lead to change of a violent nature. A hard lesson to be learned in Ulster is that civilised standards of life are thin and fragile. Others, therefore, could well look to Ulster and say "there but for the grace of God go we." So, in the face of a worldwide climate which to say the least is volatile, museums of whatever kind could consider their social significance and re-examine their policies in relation not only to what is, but to what could well be.

My concern today has been with folk museums, but where social significance is concerned, they hold no monopoly. Whether museums be those which reveal man to himself, illustrate his place in nature, or specialise in his achievements as a creative artist, a craftsman or a technician, they are all significant in the defence of civilised standards and in assisting the raising of those standards to greater heights. Social significance implies, amongst other things, reaction to social change and it must be borne in mind that social change does not always imply change for the better. Man's real enemy is his ignorance, and we still have a long way to go before it ceases to be a threat to all that man at his best holds precious.

Sources

1. Kenneth Hudson: *A Social History of Museums,* London 1975 p. 9.
2. Kenneth Hudson: *Museums for the 1980's,* UNESCO, Paris, 1977 p. 1.
3. A. T. Q. Stewart: *The Narrow Ground, Aspects of Ulster 1609-1969,* London, 1977 pp. 15-16.
4. J. H. Fabre: *The Wonders of Instinct,* 1918 p. 291.
5. G. B. Thompson: *A Museum's Role in a Changing Society,* Museums Journal, vol. 78, No. 1, June 1978, pp. 2-4.

National Maritime
Museum Barge House
*Prince Frederick's Barge,
cabin.*

Making museums market orientated

Neil Cossons

Neil Cossons is a leading authority on museums and industrial history and conservation. He started his museum career in 1961 and subsequently held posts in Bristol and Liverpool. In 1971 he became the first Director of the Ironbridge Gorge Museum, Britain's leading museum of industrial history and archaeology and in 1983 was appointed Director of the National Maritime Museum, London.

He is a past President of the Museums Association and the Association for Industrial Archaeology and currently President of the Association of Independent Museums.

He has published and broadcast widely on the subjects of museums, industrial archaeology and conservation.

"Museums are about things not people."
"What on earth have museums got to do with the needs of the public?"
"The last thing a museum should think about is giving the public what it wants."
"Museums are there to collect and conserve; the interests of the visitor are irrelevant."
"The only people who know anything about museums are curators and collectors."

In extracting this small sample from my growing collection of curatorial quotes, I have, for obvious reasons, maintained the anonymity of the speakers but all five of these statements were made quite openly and seriously in gatherings where museum professionals talk to one another.

To me they reflect a serious state of affairs, a threat to museums and all they represent in terms of curatorship, of conservation and of the standards of scholarship which should lie at the heart of what any sound museum is there to pursue. If we are charitable we can say that they reflect a misunderstanding of the relationship which can, and I believe should, exist between a museum and its users. If we are not – and there is a significant body of reasonably informed public opinion which is less than charitably disposed to the sort of people who work in museums – then we see a disdain for the public and for any sense of obligation or of service to the museum user.

Let us be charitable. Museums are clearly there primarily to collect things, to know

41

about them and to care for them and for very sound reasons by tradition they have employed people – curators – with the specialist skills necessary to carry out these functions. However, even this statement begs a number of questions for as our awareness of the remedial and preventative conservation requirements of museum collections has grown in recent years, there has been a questioning of whether the curator's attitude or knowledge is appropriate to ensure the proper physical treatment of the objects in his care. I am a passionate believer that museums should be run by curators and that curators are fundamental to the proper functioning of the museum. But having said that, I have to admit that curators are often their own worst enemies and that if museums and curators are to survive into the next century, then there has to be a fundamental reappraisal of the functions of both and the way in which one relates to the other. This is not the forum for that debate but I feel sure that many of the apparent problems of museums stem from the attitudes of curators and that had those attitudes not grown up, there would be no need for conferences with such heretical titles as "Museums are for people...."!

How has this happened? Firstly it stems from the origins of many of our great collections which, although they may have been started for reasons of curiosity and perhaps little else, in the main developed within the context of the advancing scholarship of the day. This point cannot be overstressed. In virtually all the fields of traditional museum collecting the collections themselves – at the time they were being acquired – were fundamental to the evolving scholarship of the respective subject area. The cutting edge of research in the biological sciences, in geology, in archaeology, in ethnology was based upon collections in museums, research carried out either by first-class scholars who were curators of those collections or scholars who saw the museum and what it contained as the fountain from which their knowledge derived. I do not think that it is too much of a generalisation to suggest that in many areas museums may be repositories not only of the unfashionable, but also of the irrelevant and that the epicentre of research lies elsewhere. If curators are feeling rather like an endangered species, who can be surprised if their attitude is over-protective and self-centred with strong tendencies to fall back upon "professional ethics". As I have said on a number of previous occasions when a profession starts to hide behind a code of practice, it is the interest of the user that suffers. I make this point at some length because I believe it lies at the heart of this dilemma about museums and who uses them. Museums are used by people whom curators think should use them and that is dependent upon the current aspirations, ambitions and perceptions of curators. This attitudinal factor has, I believe, been more significant in colouring the popular view of what a museum is than the collections that those museums contain.

If we look now at the use of museums by visitors (who in most museums are numerically the largest sector of users), again we see a situation in which a century or more ago the stuff of museums, when put before the public in showcases with not particularly informative labels, was immensely fascinating and satisfying to the

Prince Frederick's barge (1732), National Maritime Museum, London.

large majority of people who came in through the door. Here the ordinary man had free access to the wonders of the world. All the museum had to do was to open its doors. So why should we think differently today, why do museums need to be market-orientated and what does that mean anyway? There are two major reasons. Firstly, the museum no longer has a monopoly of vivid images and exciting experiences, for although its collections have not changed and nor has its fundamental purpose, public attitudes have. Secondly, in an increasingly mobile society with disposable time, income and discrimination, increased choice means that people are demanding quality of presentation and quality of treatment when spending their own time and money. The day of the take-it-or-leave-it museum is over. Furthermore, what is true of popular visitor attitudes to museums is increasingly true of the attitudes of those who use the other services provided by the museum, scholars who require access to curators, collections or reading rooms, enquirers, teachers, picture researchers and so on. The thirst on the part of the public at large for what the museum can and should provide is for access, for quality, for personal attention, politeness, cleanliness, efficiency, value for money, for visibly responsible and professional collections' management, in short for all those qualities that museums have not been particularly expert at

43

providing in the past. Museums will stand or fall not only by their competence to care for collections, but by their ability to care for people. In other words, they need to be market-orientated if they are to survive, if they are to command not only the respect of the taxpayer or ratepayer or visitor, who may or may not have to pay at the door, but the willingness of those users to provide the funds which museums need. If any curator thinks that society owes him a living, he is not only in for a lifetime of disappointment, but his failure to recognise that he owes something to society is a fundamental denial of curatorial principles because it poses a real threat to his museum's ability to do its job properly.

The concept of a market-orientated museum is treated with great suspicion by many curators. This is a failing stemming partly from their upbringing, partly for the historical reasons I have already outlined, but also from a misunderstanding amounting in some cases to gross ignorance about the implications of developing a market-related strategy. Put simply, marketing is the matching of a product to the potential customer for that product. If the product is not the right one, provided at the right price (which, I must emphasise, is not implying that there should be an admission charge!) and presented to the customer in the right way, then there will be no users. Sadly, in the case of museums there has been an unconscious conspiracy between curator and customer which has denied almost all these basic principles of supply and demand. On the one hand, museum curators think, not always with any justification, that they know what the customer should have or what they are

prepared to go out of their way to provide. On the other, the user, who in the case of the casual visitor to a free admission town-centre museum, may be responding to the most minimal of motivations, has a quite astonishingly low expectation and tolerance of what is provided. The curator does not need to find out what the museum user wants because he can get away with not doing. People will always trickle in through the doors if he bothers to open them. If they go away inspired or dulled by the experience, he need never know because their reaction is never recorded or measured. Furthermore, I am regretfully compelled to the view that the quality of free access, combined with the anonymity of what is for most visitors a casual and almost totally passive experience, successfully insulates the curator from his users to the dis-benefit of both. In other words, I believe that the long-standing and honourable tradition of free admission to museums, defended with such vigour by many curators, places upon their shoulders an additional responsibility towards the market, a responsibility which can only be met by a determined market policy and a real belief that museums are for people. Cuarators have to *earn the right* to provide their customers with "free" museums because if free access equates with poor quality they are directly and indirectly placing their collections at risk. When people are actually fed up with the raw deal they get from museums which provide their service "free", something is radically wrong.

But curators are not entirely to blame. The quality of service that many museums provide is often determined by factors outside their control. Lunatic opening

*Figureheads: the 74-gun
Blenheim (1813), National
Maritime Museum, London.*

*The 74-gun Hogue (1811),
National Maritime Museum,
London.*

hours are an example, where council or government policy, employment conditions and unwillingness to pay overtime can erode as much as 50 per cent of the very hours in a year when the majority of people can use what the museum has to offer. It is no accident that those museums which are open most (i.e. for 2,700 hours or more a year) are, I think without exception, independent, market-orientated museums who are masters of their own destiny. Clearly commercial opportunity succeeds where professional ideals, intentions and platitudes have failed. (I am ashamed to direct a museum that is closed on Good Friday and May Day when several thousand people will rattle the gates of the National Maritime Museum in their efforts to get in. If they want my museum that much, then they should have it.)

We are now beginning to build up a picture of how museums can become more market-orientated. Firstly, there is the question of curatorial attitude, secondly there is the ability of the museum's management to run the museum in the manner that they might wish. Neither is easy to change. In the case of the curator there needs to be a radical reappraisal of the way in which he is trained, emphasising the concept of service and responsibility to the public and ensuring that the curator has a real understanding of who the public are. I have long been of the view that all museum "professional" staff should "serve their time" during their training, working with the museum's public, in galleries as guides or demonstrators, perhaps working as attendants in uniform, manning information desks or shops, working in the Enquiry Service, manning the Reading Room, anything that generates an understanding of *who* museums are for and that creates that essential quality of humility which places the needs of the customer first. It is, I believe, no generalisation to suggest that one of our most serious failings as a nation is to place an invisible but nevertheless very real stigma upon the act of service which many people feel, quite wrongly, degrades them in their own eyes and in the eyes of those whom they serve. That generalisation does not apply in, for example, the United States where the quality of people who provide a direct service to the public is often so high. "Have a nice day" may slip easily from the lips but there are many museums in this country where I would dearly like to hear those words!

Related to curatorial attitude is market research which, I am convinced, is as important for museums, whether they are free or whether they charge admission, as it is for any other organisation that provides a service to the public. How can a museum serve a public which it does not understand? And, while a good curator will have an intuitive view of whom his museum is serving, there is I believe an increasing need to identify the various sectors of users if only to determine whether the museum is making contact effectively with the society it is supposed to be serving.

The lessons of market research can be applied in a wide variety of ways, not only in terms of the quality of what the museum provides directly to its customers but as a persuasive weapon in convincing a Board of Trustees or Committee of Management that the museum must up its game. If museums are to truly service their public, then those responsible for managing them must be given the opportunity to manage, to determine the strategy and tactics of the museum in relationship to the museum's real needs. This clearly poses problems for the majority of museums which inevitably tend to reflect in their methods of operation, broader policies which are not always relevant to their direct needs. In this context museums are much closer to the performing arts than they are to the more mundane services provided by, for example, a local authority. A museum is a programme-related activity and the more sensitive it is to the needs of its users, the more it needs the freedom and the management structure necessary to devise and operate responsively. In the case, for example, of our national museums, all of which now have trustee status, I am firmly of the view that they must be freed from the more restrictive apron strings of Government. Let the trustees get on with the job as they think fit so that these museums can devise and adapt their own specialised systems to exploit every opportunity for self-help on the one hand and respond to the needs of the user on the other. There is no reason for them all to conform to structures devised outside their walls; on the contrary, the differences are greater than the similarities, and necessity is a great mother of invention. Self-help and market-awareness go hand-in-hand but neither can happen without freedom of action. Provide the opportunity and these museums will quickly evolve and, I believe, substantially improve the quality of what they do for their users. None of this need prejudice scholarship and research. On the contrary, the very provision of high quality services for visitors and all other categories of users will further the trend towards selectivity and discrimination on the part of the public at large.

I have perhaps paid undue attention to the popular face of the museum. But there is a real and growing demand for the specialist and scholarly services which a museum provides. The need for market awareness is no less relevant in these areas and museums must increasingly examine the way in which they handle enquiries, the quality of their documentation systems, in short, all those aspects of their work which provide access to their collections. An implication of increased market awareness is the adaptation of the product to satisfy the requirements of the user. This need in no way be a threat to those real and worthwhile traditional values which many museums represent. It need not mean vulgarisation nor a dilution of quality but it inevitably means a much more explicit statement of what the museum is able to provide. How rarely one sees a museum advertising opportunities for research or promoting the existence of its Enquiry Service. More frequently enquiry answering is restricted, as is access to curators, who presumably have more important things to occupy them. All of this brings me back to the question of attitude and a re-statement of the belief that the laws of supply and demand, of a matching of product to market, are as relevant to a museum and the value placed upon the intangible services which it provides as they are to those who supply the more concrete necessities of life. A failure to recognise the needs of the user poses perhaps the greatest threat to a museum's collections.

Stirling Smith Art Gallery and Museum: children examining their finds after a "mini beast" hunt during Operation Skylark, 1983.

48

Making a museum work

Deborah Haase

Deborah Haase was born in Glasgow. She studied
archaeology and medieval history at Glasgow
University and subsequently took a post graduate
course in the museum studies department at
Leicester University. Her first professional
engagement was in Kirkintilloch, where she set up
the award-winning Strathkelvin District Museum
Service. Since 1982, as curator of the Stirling Smith
Art Gallery and Museum, she has supervised its
reopening, staffing, and reorganisation with the
intention of creating a museum, art gallery and
centre for the arts in the area.

I remember when I first went to Stirling Smith Art Gallery and Museum, I was faced with a virtually derelict building and a museum that received little more than a handful of visitors. It was struggling to survive years of closure and many more years of physical neglect with a staff of two and a budget best described as minimal. In fact it was quite clear that most people did not know Stirling had a museum and those who had visited best remembered the chalk circles on the floor which, believe it or not, marked where containers should be placed on rainy days.

Clearly work at the Smith and making the Smith work was going to be challenging – and so it has proved to be. In a nutshell, what we had to do was catch up on the yesterdays, function today and plan for the tomorrows; and that applied to work behind the scenes and in the public view.

We would need money, we would need staff and we would need resources.

We tackled our problems by assessing our situation, identifying our future intentions and recognising what was expected of us. That essential ground work allied to a sound theoretical approach, support from colleagues on the staff and elsewhere and through seeking additional assistance from the Scottish Museums Council, the Manpower Services Commission, the Scottish Tourist Board and other bodies has allowed us to make considerable progress over the last 18 months or so.

Now museum workers learn quite correctly that their primary duty is to the collections in their care. Many of our older museums, like the Smith, arose out of private bequests, closed societies or through association with academic institutions.

With assured, albeit modest incomes, they concentrated on collecting, conservation and research. As a result the need for management skills and the acknowledgement of the needs of the uninformed public were often overlooked.

More recently, we have seen the development of a wider range of museums. Today contemporary non-national museums tend to be either plurally-funded independents, or local authority museums. They have been forced to compete for public or private funding to ensure their survival and, as a result, have often found themselves subject to additional pressures. Local authority museums can suffer from too close an association with library or other leisure and recreation functions with whom they have to vie for staff, resources and attention. Plurally-funded museums run the risk of being subjected to too close an economically based scrutiny from hard-headed business sponsors. Clearly there is now an imperative duty on all museums to demonstrate their efficiency and abilities to undertake accurate and efficient physical and fiscal planning. Consequently, today's museums have found it necessary to emphasise different functions from those of the older museums. These developments have contributed to the necessity for museum staff to come down from their ivory towers, acknowledge their public dependence and provide a service in return for investment.

The problems at the Smith were particular but by no means unique. We had to balance our over-riding duty to the collections with the expectations of our employers and public who were anxious to see the museum open and the building in use. By employing our theoretical framework we were equipped to articulate and combine professional requirements with the aspirations of our governing committee.

We committed ourselves to becoming an open museum as soon as possible and set about creating a situation in which we could strengthen the active input of other parties – employees, volunteers and the community – in the life of the museum. This necessity to define the role of the museum in relation to the community complemented the ideas and hopes of both the staff and the governing committee.

With the museum closed during the previous ten years there was basically no community or visitor habit of museum-going in Stirling so the decision to reopen as soon as possible meant we had to make the best use of the limited spaces available: we had to ensure that while visitors could not have access to the whole building that they would be sufficiently satisfied to find their visit worthwhile.

Identifying potential visitors was not difficult. Children are a prime target group we wish to encourage into the museum realising the additional benefit we can gain of parental interest if the children are stimulated. Tourist and specialist interest groups are other obvious targets. We had to take into consideration the fact that Stirling welcomes huge numbers of visitors during the summer – we would not be able to grow slowly – and we would have to train staff and visitors to use the museum which was a new and strange environment for them.

Mary Louise Coulouris, printmaker in residence at Stirling Smith Art Gallery and Museum working with a school group. Complementing the Scottish Museums Council exhibition Piranesi: Views of Rome, *school groups were able to work with the printmaker using techniques similar to those used in the 18th century.*

So what have we done over the last two years? We actively campaigned for staff and volunteers to start to make the Smith work again. We have got ourselves a working budget and increased the full-time staff from two to six and part-time staff from 2¼ to 4½. We have upgraded the entrance hall and installed a much-needed local history display, along with a reception and sales area. Our natural history room has been upgraded to take temporary exhibitions. The original watercolour gallery has been restored and presently houses temporary exhibitions including ones drawn from our own collections. The former ethnography gallery is now a theatre, and a workshop and stores have been created and fitted out in what was once the main museum gallery. Most recently the curator's flat has been converted to house offices, library and staff room and additional security provision has been installed.

We use temporary exhibitions to attract differing interest groups in the community. We organise complementary educational and other activities. For example, "Pay Peanuts and get Monkeys" was our opening exhibition last June. This exhibition on unemployment was devised, researched and created jointly by museum staff and local unemployed people.

A touring exhibition "Archaeology's Action Men" prompted us to arrange our own exhibition of local archaeological material, an essay competition for children and a display forum for local and national archaeological societies and organisations. With the assistance of the Education Officer of the National Museum of Antiquities we organised a teachers' workshop, provided a reading list, objects for handling and worksheets for teachers to use. In addition we made arrangements for visiting school groups to have the opportunity of meeting the Regional Archaeologist to hear and discuss her work.

In conjunction with a recent exhibition on contemporary studio ceramics we invited a potter to take up residence in the museum theatre. Visitors were able to discuss his work and aspects of working with clay. Special arrangements were made to allow groups from schools to come and work with him while in another part of the theatre visitors could watch a series of video films on the art of the potter. Visitors have expressed their appreciation of the combined exhibition and activities and particularly gratifying are the visits to this and other exhibitions by groups of school children – their visit to the Smith is often the first they have made to any museum or gallery.

We actively organise for children. We actively seek to involve other agencies in the work of the museum. An example of this was Operation Skylark – a tripartite co-operative venture between the museum, the Countryside Ranger Service and the Scottish Conservation Volunteers. The week long playscheme with a conservation theme based in and around the museum was one of the star events of the 1983 Stirling Festival, repeated again last year by popular request. The project introduced 100 children and their parents to the museum each day. Project costs were met by local and national sponsorship and the 40 or so adult volunteers came throughout the Region. Publicity? The local Press provided this free and the project was chosen for inclusion in television coverage of the

hopefully by the restoration of our main gallery space.

As you can see community involvement is encouraged in diverse ways. In addition to some of those already mentioned, the museum has provided rehearsal and workshop space for theatre groups and recently even provided the backdrop for a couple's wedding day photographs. Our aim is to make our museum invaluable and available to our community in as many ways as possible.

By seeking out extra money and assistance we have been able to stretch our small budget, allowing a more dynamic progress than would otherwise have been possible. Visitor numbers have increased by up to 84 per cent in 1983 and a further 25 per cent last year. We have attracted a large number of children into the museum, and hopefully, started to create in them a basis of museum users of the future. We have increased the public's awareness of the museum – the local newspaper serving as the most valuable medium for informing the public and councillors about the museum and what it is trying to do. We have received recognition from within the profession with the award presented in the 1984 Scottish Museum of the Year Awards scheme.

Making the Smith start to work again has required total commitment and enthusiasm from all the staff. We hope progress towards full opening will continue so that the Smith can develop its traditional and new-found rôles in the community. Certainly there is less of yesterday's dereliction evident, the museum is open today and plans for tomorrow are in hand.

Festival. An exhibition after the project displayed the children's handicrafts, explained the aims of the project and provided a further opportunity to publicly recognise volunteer and sponsor support.

Following the restoration of two galleries we decided that our next priority should be the creation of the theatre. With flexible seating to allow multi-purpose use, this space allows us to develop the complementary, educational and live aspects to exhibitions as well as providing a meeting place for local groups and a pleasant venue for drama, music and theatre events. In line with this policy our priority now is the creation of a café which is seen as an integral part of the development of the museum to be followed

Spartan, last of the Kirkintilloch-built puffers, launched in 1942 and now preserved by the Scottish Maritime Museum.

Building a public for a new museum

Campbell McMurray

Campbell McMurray was born in Scotland and grew up in Campbeltown, Argyllshire. He undertook an engineering apprenticeship and then had four to five years seafaring. After leaving university he joined the staff of the National Maritime Museum, London as Caird Research Fellow – an oral history project on ancient seafarers. He joined their full-time staff in the mid-1970s in the Department of Printed Volumes and Manuscripts. In 1979 he became Assistant Keeper and in 1983 left to become Director of the Scottish Maritime Museum.

Scotland has significantly lagged behind the rest of the UK in the development of museums based around industrial themes, such as those at Beamish, Ironbridge or the Black Country Museum. The impetus to establish industrial museums probably got under way in the 1950s, gathering pace in England and Wales in the later 1960s and early 1970s.

The position in Scotland is quite radically different, and while there is no occasion here to rehearse the sorry saga of this country's neglect of its industrial heritage, not just in comparison with what was happening elsewhere but in relation to the provision for other respects of the heritage north of the border, it must be said that until quite recent years national policy towards the establishment of industrial museums was not well-developed. The picture is now changing, of course, and one can only welcome this new dawning.

Within this picture of neglect and under-development, it has to be conceded that, as far as the protection and preservation of Scotland's maritime heritage is concerned, the Scottish Maritime Museum has missed the early morning tide – this both in relation to materials, objects, ephemera etc., and in the context of the prevailing economic climate, which could not in any circumstances be judged to be a hospitable setting for the aspirations which we have for the Irvine project.

Long before the Museum was conceived, radical structural changes in the pattern of industry in Scotland as a whole, but particularly in the shipbuilding and heavy engineering sectors and in the shipping trade more generally, had conspired to sweep away huge areas of the country's maritime and industrial heritage. Yet, still much remained and, with the application of consummate amounts of energy and the

Model of the Irvine Harbour redevelopment scheme showing the new slipway, winch house, wharf and floating pontoons, projects carried out by Irvine Development Corporation for the Scottish Maritime Museum.

readiness to tackle the very real and quite singular problems which the preservation of this heavy technology poses for the museum curator – and with the continuing support of the Development Corporation at Irvine in the provision of a solid capital infrastructure – results to date have exceeded expectations to quite an extraordinary degree. And the Scottish Maritime Museum is now widely regarded as the rightful custodian of Scotland's maritime heritage.

The question of financial support for the new undertaking is altogether more problematic. In general, the justification for the existence of museums in society is rooted not in narrowly conceived economic terms but, rather, rests on intrinsic cultural, social, educational, environmental or other grounds, and on the benefits to a community which might accrue or otherwise be generated by the presence of such an establishment in a given locale – e.g. improved employment prospects and

Winch house and entrance of the new slipway and wharf at Irvine Harbour, Scottish Maritime Museum.

increased job opportunities generally; growth of income per head from prospective visitor spending; focal point for volunteer and community effort, etc.

Notwithstanding such advantages, it has always been, and all the evidence would suggest that it will continue to be, a struggle for museums to survive, to finance their capital programmes and cover their operating and maintenance costs. The extent of the financial support which museums receive is, of course, variable: local authority and national museums have been traditionally subsidised virtually 100 per cent.

Independent museums, whatever their objectives or themes could only, in almost all cases, have come into existence with the hidden support of, most usually, enlightened public corporations or occasionally, beneficent individuals. Site acquisitions, access and preparation and other landscaping costs are effectively

concealed or may be pushed through under another umbrella, such as land reclamation or environmental rehabilitation programmes. Major developments in the independent industrial museum field, in particular, are really only possible given substantial and continuing – uncertain – support from the Manpower Services Commission (MSC), functioning as the primary source for the supply of labour.

In our own 35-person MSC Community Programme Scheme now operational at Irvine, the contribution from MSC in the form of salaries and other allowances is in excess of £125,000 for the year. At other establishments, where the MSC numbers might extend to as many as 200-plus, the equivalent figure will exceed £700,000 per annum. This represents a colossal source of financial support; but even allowing for this and for the fact that we are most likely to be able to write off the heavy start-up capital costs, the burdensome demands of continuing capital works will require that strenuous efforts be made in the field of fund-raising and other methods of private sponsorship. For certain kinds of industrial museums, for example mining museums, capital costs are likely to be very high while operating costs will be similarly heavy, given the high cost of maintenance and the need to observe stringent safety standards.[1]

In any event, the Scottish Maritime Museum in common with existing and proposed industrial museum undertakings will inevitably be dependent to a significant extent on admission receipts as a source of operating revenue. The questions therefore posed by the title of this paper are extremely apposite: building a public for a new museum – where is one to find this public? How is one to attract it into the Scottish Maritime Museum?

More problematically, perhaps, how is one to induce this public which is both more discriminating and more sensitive to its right to quality of service, to make regular return visits?

In the first place, clearly we must be able to offer something that the public wants; we must in different words have a "product to market". Existing industrial museums appear to have enjoyed a popular success based on one or other, or on a blend, of the following: –

1. Situated on an historic site –
   e.g. Ironbridge.
2. Traditional industrial processes taking place in situ – e.g. Gladstone Pottery Museum.
3. Reconstruction of industrial and social history – e.g. Beamish.
4. The collection of items around a theme – e.g. National Tramway Museum, Crich.

In relation to the marketing of the product, it would seem that there are three main areas or points of appeal:

a) A genuine focus for the establishment which has both legitimate museological and educational value;

b) The opportunity to witness people at work in an historical setting, or in an historically authentic reconstruction;

c) The chance for visitors to participate in some aspect of the activity – such as riding in a steam train or, in the case of a

mining museum, to share the "underground experience".[2]

I wish to return to these criteria in due course, and the manner in which I believe that we have met most of them at Irvine, but initially it can be said that the museum in search of a public must be capable of offering a satisfactory, and satisfying, blend of education and entertainment.

At approximately this juncture I should be placing before you a dazzling array of graphs, histograms and bar charts demonstrating such things as the likely frequency distribution of the ages, educational attainment, sex, occupations etc., of the future Scottish Maritime Museum visiting public, together with little maps illustrating their probable geographical scatter, a note or two on the likely duration of their visit to the Museum, and I should have concluded with some estimate of the likelihood of their making return visits. This I am afraid I cannot do. Indeed, to measure the characteristics and preferences of any existing museum's visiting public is a daunting enough task, one which only a handful have tried; to attempt it for a museum which does not yet have a public would call surely for a knowledge of the occult!

But while such empirical data would undoubtedly be of value in determining broad areas of development for a new museum,[3] it would be an imprudent management which sought to elaborate the identity and collecting policies of its establishment, the character of its displays and their overall presentation, simply on the basis of what the public thought it wanted of a museum. It would hardly be a

Irvine, Harbour, c. 1903, looking down river from the site of the new Scottish Maritime Museum slipway.

Scottish Maritime Museum, Irvine: the almost completed pontoons constructed for mooring the Museum's vessels, 1984.

museum at all, indeed. To qualify for this distinction there has to be present in the first place a coherent, well-thought out and museologically sound philosophy or viewpoint underpinning the enterprise, together with some firm notion of the position in the wider scheme of things which the new foundation was seeking to occupy. That is to say, initial conception, planning and policy making in a new museum is always to some extent, by definition, a subjective exercise – an act of faith, even.

Stating the position as briefly as circumstances will permit, it can be said that the sea, ships and seafaring in all their aspects run like a golden thread through the history of Scotland and her people. The failure of a past generation to initiate a national museum to reflect and express the far-reaching contribution of the Scots to the maritime life in all its facets is a matter for profound regret. The reasons for this costly omission are complex and need not detain us here. The Scottish Maritime Museum Trust (Irvine) was set up in 1983 precisely to remedy the deficiency. The principal aim of the Trust is to establish a museum to collect, research, conserve and to display something of the rich and diverse character of the Scottish maritime heritage, and to preserve a portion of this inheritance for future generations.

The advent of the Scottish Maritime Museum is very much part of a more general development in Scotland which has seen the emergence of the individual thematic or industry-based collections, itself the product in some degree of the relative failure of the existing national collections to attend adequately to the preservation of the industrial heritage. Within this emerging collective – which would include the Scottish Fisheries Museum at Anstruther; the Prestongrange Mining Museum; the Museum of Wool Textiles at Walkerburn; the Lead Mining Museum at Wanlockhead; the various railway preservation society schemes, and the splendid New Lanark conservation project – the Scottish Maritime Museum has its office. While recognising the contribution of other establishments within the field – notably at Anstruther, for fishing; the fine ship model collections, at Glasgow Museum of Transport; and the equally splendid nautical instruments and models of the Royal Scottish Museum – the Scottish Maritime Museum seeks to express in the widest possible fashion the contribution of Scotland's maritime industries to the history and cultural evolution of her people. As John Hume writes,

"Scotland's contribution to the world during the last quarter of a millenium has been distinguished out of proportion to the numbers of her inhabitants. The influence, not only of engineers and shipbuilders of Clydeside, but of those involved in linen, cotton, jute and woollen textiles, of iron-smelters and papermakers and more recently in electronics and oil has been far-reaching and pervasive. Theirs is a proud heritage, and the time is long overdue for telling, in terms of objects, buildings, structures and images of the triumphs, and the reverses, of those who created a vital part of the culture of the nation".[4]

It is precisely here then, in defining and expressing the maritime component of this great cultural heritage that we find the genuine museological, intellectual and educational basis for the Scottish Maritime Museum.

Although it possesses certain disadvantages, and in no way compares with, for example, Ironbridge as a site of primary historical importance, the town of Irvine makes a perfectly appropriate home for the Scottish Maritime Museum. The only New Town beside the sea, Irvine is in fact an ancient Royal Burgh which enjoyed a prosperous history as a leading Scottish port from around the end of the 17th century until the early decades of the present one. It was the third port in the kingdom, indeed until the deepening of the Clyde towards the end of the 18th century robbed it of this distinction. Shipbuilding was carried on in the town throughout moste of the 19th century, coming to an end only in the middle of the 1930s, when the grass was growing in a great many shipyards. Ship repairing, however, continued and drew to a close only in the 1960s. Comprising a wide range of bulksome commodities including coal, limestone, timber and other housebuilding materials and, as time went on, explosives to an increasing degree, and other chemical goods, the cargo traffic of the port was typical of many in the British Isles in the extent to which it reflected, in this particular part of the country, the development of the industrial economy.[5] But by the end of the 1960s or so, with activity in the port overall reduced to a mere shadow of its former substance, much of the harbour wharfage and its attendant facilities fell into disuse and decay. Today, only a small and, predictably, declining export of explosives from the river continues.

With this decline, the harbour area as a whole lost a good deal of its former vitality, while developments elsewhere in the town worked to shift the centre of gravity of the community away from the waterside. Nevertheless, in spite of the spreading dereliction, sufficient of the fabric of the area remained to encourage the Development Corporation to embark on its rehabilitation programme in the early 1980s. In addition to the implementation of the initial proposals for the Museum in and around the harbour, the works included restoration of the existing properties and the re-instatement of the razed housing by new building in the vernacular style, developments which have done much to rejuvenate this formerly neglected neighbourhood.

Not less important in this progress have been the large-scale public works which have led to the reclamation of vast tracts of wasteland, transforming these into a splendid area known as the Beach Park and leading to the construction of the hugely popular and mammoth Magnum Leisure Centre. These and related developments – most recently, plans have been approved for the construction of a sea-life and underwater interpretation centre – taken together point the direction along which further improvements will take place, viz., towards the creation of a new rôle for this erstwhile industrial town, one based this time to a predominant extent on leisure, recreation and tourism. And it is in this overall context that the establishment of the Scottish Maritime Museum at Irvine must at base be seen. In different words, at an elementary but by no means negligible level, from the viewpoint of building up a public for the new establishment, it must

be considered that we begin with certain advantages.

Thus while Irvine has not hitherto been considered as exactly the jewel in the North Ayrshire crown, its situation within a mere 25 miles of the chief population centre in Scotland and almost precisely in the middle of a well-established and popular tourist area is of enormous significance for the Museum; add to this the fact that we share an operating environment in which leisure and recreational pursuits constitute a large and growing element, and it must appear that at least in theory there exists a prospective audience for the Scottish Maritime Museum.

While proximity to a large population catchment area, which we at Irvine enjoy, would seem on the face of it to be an obvious advantage, the relationship if any between that and visitor attendance is an elusive one. But what does seem to emerge clearly is that there are distinct gains in being well-located in a tourist area. This naturally produces a strong seasonal influence in visitor attendance.

Almost all studies of visitor attendance in museums, both in this country – relatively few, admittedly – and abroad tend to point up the characteristic seasonal profile of museum visiting: viz., the "seven weeks and seven days" syndrome. Three fairly distinct peaks are easily discernible – one in April, associated with the Easter and other Bank Holidays; similarly evident but less marked in March, when Easter falls early; the second and main peak takes place in July and August, coinciding with national school, industrial and commercial holidays; and there is typically a third peak, around October or November, not so easily explained, but probably associated with the first term of the new school and university year.[6]

The Scottish Maritime Museum would not anticipate any marked departure from this trend, although we are aware of the implications for management – the extensive use of voluntary support in the summer months, for example – which it implies. As with other museums, we would naturally expect school visits and other educational excursions to comprise a substantial proportion of the total visitor numbers. It would be rash at this stage to predict with too much force just what proportion of the whole we might expect from this source; but in a new foundation, occupying a field of wide social and historical interest, such an educational resource as we are planning at Irvine could generate up to one-third or perhaps 40 per cent of the total number of visitors in each year, and here proximity to a large catchment area does presumably have an effect. In the meantime, we are currently hard at work laying down the groundwork in this important area, preparing

pamphlets, worksheets etc., and trying to devise schemes which will make the best use of our resources while at the same time seeking to provide ways of adding to the occasion of the individual's visit. That is to say, we are endeavouring to do more than merely duplicate, in the case of schoolchildren, what the schools are already offering. Our view rests on the belief that a visit to a museum should be an experience, an answer to the dominance of the school timetable; going to a museum, in different words, we feel, ought to mean going to a special place for a special event, or series of events, which should be at least as stimulating as the bus journey which precedes the visit![7]

Our first practical effort in education will be a series of 20 evening classes in a maritime history workshop, commencing this autumn, in which the chief focus will be on the use of original sources, but not merely documents. The bulk of the course will involve the use of guest lecturers, not academics as a rule, but local people of maritime background – shipmasters, shipowners, shipbrokers, shipwrights, and so on – who will, by way of oral history interviewing conducted by myself, speak to the class about themselves, their work and their lives in the shipping trade, thereby bringing directly into the museum something of the colour, vigour and character of their personal experience. We would naturally hope to publish the results of this workshop. In terms of building up a public for the new museum, this would also have the merit of connecting us more firmly into the local community. Such approaches I see as being merely the opening round in our approach to the museum and education – the range of other possibilities in addition to the more standard fare is limitless, and to define them too explicitly would be to limit them. They could include simple occasions, such as the individual craftsman talking about his work and the development of his skills; the dialogue where two views on the same subject are expounded; many more methods, involving other means of communication in which music and dramatic gesture could play a part, also, suggest themselves.

The subject of education in museums is a large one, meriting closer attention than it as a rule receives. But if we are genuinely committed in our intentions and truly wish to build up an intelligent, informed, thoughtful and questing public, with an appetite for museums then the matter is one which we need to explore from every side. After all,

> "... we have a declared interest in our subjects and it is impossible to define the limits of that interest. We are committed to the belief that certain things are valuable and worth preserving and it seems a logical consequence of that view that we should wish to provide further information about such things by all the means at our disposal ..."[8]

The viewpoint is one which we wholeheartedly endorse at the Scottish Maritime Museum. Its successful realisation in practice we see as being among the most important elements in the building up of a public for our museum.

I have suggested that the museum in search of a public, if it is to succeed, must offer a blend of education and entertainment. It must, in other words,

address itself directly to the task of satisfying both the specialist interests of the genuinely committed visitor, the minority – for whom the purpose of the visit will be a combination of research, education and interpretation – as well as the more general interests of the casual visitor, who will be in the majority and for whom an enjoyable, uncomplicated, not too intellectually demanding visit will probably be the most that is expected, given a relatively strong basic product, offering both educational stimulus and an enjoyable, even memorable experience, the growth of interest from Tourist Boards, other supporting agencies and the media could all work to promote further development and expansion. Marketing and promotion are obviously of the most critical importance, particularly where financial circumstances dictate a need to attract large numbers of visitors paying relatively high charges.

While this need not be frightfully expensive, and could depend greatly on one's success in wooing the media, it does above all require that we have something to market. Just as any other service has to justify itself at some point on the basis of what exactly it can offer to the public, so with museums. In the way of the world we live in, museums have no divine right to exist. Life is going to be a continuing struggle, even in the most propitious circumstances; more so for large industrial museum developments. These difficulties will be greatly compounded if what is offered to the public is not appealing and well-constructed.

What then has the Scottish Maritime Museum to offer? The basis of our

Kyles, originally a steam coaster, built in Paisley in 1872 and acquired by the Scottish Maritime Museum in 1984.

approach rests on

"... the premise that maritime history is primarily about boats and ships. The needs, aspirations and circumstances of owners, masters, crews, and customers are realised, through designers and builders, in the design of vessels. The knowledge, experience, skills and lifestyles of these people are embodied in the physical form of each vessel. The Museum should, therefore, seek to interpret craft, the skills and equipment employed in their use and the tools and skills employed in their construction, set against the social background which produced them. The best media for this interpretation are the vessels themselves, authentically preserved, the places in which they were built, authentically reconstructed, and the skills by which they were built, kept alive. Every aspect of the Museum, visitor services, research, documentation, collection, conservation, and display, should be integrated with this approach ..."[9]

Within this ambitious framework it is possible, I think, to discern elements which meet the criteria for popular success enjoyed by existing industrial museums, as pointed to above. The proposed restoration, conservation and replication activities provide every opportunity for visitors to witness traditional maritime skills, crafts and processes in their appropriate context. The essential aims of the Museum are framed around the reconstruction of the industrial, social and commercial history of the shipping trade and its contingent activities in Scotland, arranged either by theme, subject or function.

In relation to the "marketing of the product", with reference to what has gone before, I have already drawn attention to the genuine museological and intellectual basis for the new enterprise. The opportunity which our proposals envisage for visitors to have access to the Museum workshops, which will in addition provide suitable environments for the display of wooden boatbuilding tools and other gear, will permit them to observe at first hand the use of traditional maritime skills in their authentic context. The guided visit, accompanied by worksheets and other printed matter, however, will comprise but one component in this scheme. While the organised, more passive visitor experience will continue to have a place, our intention is to provide properly structured opportunities for a more active, participative rôle in the activities of the Museum. Conditions have arisen in the modern world, and they give every indication of intensifying, which place all museums squarely in the position of responsibility for the preservation, and utilisation, of that great heritage of engineering craft skills, boatbuilding techniques, design formulas, and so on, which lay behind the technical triumphs of the past. If museums are to continue to have a meaningful function, they must extend beyond merely the collection and restoration of the artefacts of the past and pursue diligently the less tangible but infinitely more precious skills and practical techniques without which such constructs could not have appeared. Our craft heritage is a vital, living thing. It still survives, but its continued existence depends ultimately on its continuing use.

It is not enough then merely to collect antique craft and store them away. That is to provide a mere cemetery of bric-a-brac. We at the Scottish Maritime Museum are seeking to implement active programmes for the reclaiming and re-working of the inherited resources of the past, the skills, techniques and talents of the people, by way of opportunities for visitor participation in boatbuilding, replication, sail training and other related activities.

These would be available both to those fortunate enough to have sufficient leisure to learn as a recreation and to less privileged unemployed school leavers, working on training schemes. Our particular intention here, and a major plank in our marketing strategy in seeking to build up a popular appeal, would be that of a museum taking a responsible place in its community and trying to make a positive contribution to the life of that community.

Within the context of existing Government training schemes, this proposal implies that the Museum build into its operating structure a continuing and properly considered young people's training programme, which would bring benefit both to the Museum, in terms of conservation and restoration works achieved, and to the community by offering its young people interesting, creative and worthwhile employment. Given such a programme,

"... a group of 18-20 trainees under four or five supervisors could carry out an extended programme of research and practical restoration and replication, admittedly at slow speed, but with enormous benefits in terms of effort and commitment and within a framework that would demonstrate the Museum's

ability to provide something of value to the community. Such a programme could rebuild a couple of fishing boats, re-erect reclaimed buildings or machinery, or construct a number of pulling boats for use as hire boats above the weir on the River Irvine. It would be foolish to pretend that young people leaving such a scheme would inevitably find employment in a boatyard, in a museum, or at all ...

(But) certainly everyone leaving such a scheme at Irvine would do so not merely with access to a wide range of skills but with their confidence enhanced and a real sense of achievement. The Museum

Denny Ship Model Experiment Tank Building: the 350ft long test tank, looking towards the carriage.

would benefit by the increase and improvement of its collection through a continuing process of research, re-construction and replication, and gain the 'less tangible but equally valuable asset of a sense of performing a valuable role in the community . . .'" [10]

The marketing and promotion of a museum is a two-edged weapon, of course, in that every visitor has a cost, and it is vitally important to ensure that the numbers of visitors do not exceed the capacity of the operation to provide a properly satisfying and memorable visitor experience. Failure here, and we run the risk not least of jeopardising the very necessary growth of return visits. On that basis we have tended in our thinking on visitor numbers to keep our expectations within what we calculate the emerging organisation has the capacity to cope with, congruent with our hopes for the venture in terms of visitor satisfaction. The figures we have been working around pivot on the 10-20,000 for the first year or so.

In this context however, it is constructive to consider the overall trends in visitor numbers, where these are available, for those entering museums either like the Royal Scottish Museum, with specific collections of an industrial nature or thematic/subject-based establishments, such as the Museum of Scottish Lead Mining at Wanlockhead, or the Museum of Flight, East Lothian, some of which levy admission charges ranging up to £1 for adults.

There is no overall trend in numbers, although the remarkable Lead Mining Museum presents a distictly upward arcing curve, while the Royal Scottish Museum appears to be on a decline relatively. Looked at dispassionately it could be said that experience in Scotland with regard to industrial museum undertakings is neither spectacularly encouraging nor downright depressing. Visitor charges applied are relatively low compared with the average south of the border.

In any event, the conclusion must be what it has always been, namely that to sustain visitor numbers and charges at a level which the traffic on all sides will bear and hence go some way towards containing operating expenses will require that the Scottish Maritime Museum be capable of

Museums in Central Scotland [11] Visitor Numbers 1980-83				
	1980	1981	1982	1983
Doune Motor Museum	35,389	32,580	–	–
Glasgow Museum of Transport	339,209	296,039	308,426	267,421
Hamilton District Museum	23,000	22,500	–	–
Museum of Flight	16,346	17,845	24,039	24,283
Biggar Gasworks	NK	1,217	1,349	1,742
Museum of Lead Mining	20,056	23,000	28,000	30,000
Royal Scottish Museum	612,857	598,075	589,909	545,218
Scottish Fisheries Museum	42,720	35,119	38,000	40,000

offering something which has considerable visitor appeal. I happen to think that it does indeed possess this rather elusive ingredient.

If finally museums really are for people, then we must be pretty certain of what it is that we are offering them and take the greatest care to ensure that in the zealous quest to make our establishments more market-orientated (shorthand for bringing them into line with the prevailing orthodoxy) we do not lose sight of the true goal and purpose of the museum. This is still, in my view, to act as one of the chief sources and principal repositories of the clues to an understanding of our roots, of how and why we have come to be where we are, of our culture, if you will. Our primary objective then must continue to be that of seeking to forge in our public a strong sense of their cultural identity, a traditional obligation of the museum which in a world like ours, where change is the only constant, is perhaps a more vital responsibility than any other.[12]

Sources

1. *Scottish Mining Museum: Development and Marketing Study,* PEIDA, 10 Chester Street, Edinburgh, in association with Thorburn Associates, 17 Albany Street, Edinburgh, 1983.
2. *op cit,* paras 2.6-2.8.
3. The Public of the Ulster Museum : A Statistical Survey, by Philip Doughty, *Museums Journal,* Volume 68, 1968, pp47ff.
4. An Industrial Museum for Scotland, by John Hume, *The Scottish Review,* August 1982, p17.
5. *The Development of the West of Scotland Economy,* by Anthony Slaven, London, 1975, *passim.*
6. Doughty, *op cit.,* pp21-22.
7. The Museum as Neutral Ground, by Alun Williams, *Amgueddfa,* Bulletin of the National Museum of Wales, Spring 1971, p32.
8. Alun Williams, *op cit.*
9. *Scottish Maritime Museum : Draft Development Plan,* January 1983, by John MacAuley and Stephen Kay, unpublished.
10. *Training in the Scottish Maritime Museum,* July 1982 by Stephen Kay, an unpublished paper.
11. *STB Visitor Survey of Individual Museums,* quoted in *Scottish Mining Museum Study,* PEIDA, et al., paras 4.5-4.8 amended and updated. Biggar Gas Works opened in 1980 and is staffed from the Royal Scottish Museum, with restricted opening, likewise the Museum of Flight.
12. *Museums and the Search for Cultural Identity,* by Henrique Abranches, paper to the 13th General Conference of ICOM, 1983.

Duane Hanson's Tourists
(Gallery of Modern Art,
Edinburgh). Any object
becomes a possible Press
picture when associated
with people – to humanise
it, enliven it, and put it in
context, both in scale and
The Scotsman
Publications Limited

The Press museums deserve

Ian Grant Cumming

Born in Inverness, Ian Grant Cumming trained and worked in newspapers and magazines in Dundee and Edinburgh, with a break of several years during which he worked in the Royal Scottish Museum in Edinburgh. He turned to public relations work in 1970, and as Scottish Ballet's first Press officer, was responsible for establishing the Company's name and image as the national ballet company. In 1974 he set up his own business in Edinburgh – the only PR consultancy in Scotland to specialise in the arts. His services have been retained by the Scottish Philharmonic Society, the Royal Lyceum Theatre and many others in the fields of music, dance and publishing. His current clients include the National Galleries of Scotland (since 1979) and the Scottish Museums Council.

Museums scored higher than football matches in Scotland last year, according to figures released by the Scottish Tourist Board.

And the visitors – over 5,000,000 of them – hugely outnumbered those who went to the cinema or to performing arts events.[1]

You could argue, of course, that some of them probably came in for climatic rather than museological reasons (and a lot more where admission was free). But according to a Scottish Office survey, less than ten per cent of museum visitors admitted to coming in to shelter from the rain. Reasons like "general interest in museums and galleries" and "special interest in subject of museum or gallery" scored a comfortable

65 per cent over those who were influenced by the weather outside.[2]

Whether surveys like these bring out the truth or not is arguable (although I'm convinced that more than ten per cent of the population is honest). But the thought that they came in at all is surely the one to conjure with.

Because it means that the world "museum" is no longer synonymous in the public's mind with dust, must, and boredom.

A paragraph in a popular Scottish newspaper summed it up neatly: "Gone are the days when museums were stuffy places. Nowadays the best of them are part of the

BBC Television lining up on a mantrap in the Scottish Museums Council exhibition One for the Pot.

leisure industry, offering entertainment and a good day out".[3]

A subjective judgment? One writer's viewpoint?

It doesn't matter. To most people, the notion that "It must be true, it was in the papers" still holds good. What lies behind that is the general – if mistaken – belief in the objectivity of editorial comment.

And this is a cornerstone of public relations.

This is how it works. If a paid advertisement says an exhibition's wonderful, you

remember that's what the organisers would like you to believe. But if the Press agree, you assume it's pretty good – or at least worth a visit.

Effective use of the Press is a way of reaching many more people.

It's a circular process. "Good public relations," says Susan Lynn Davis in the American museum magazine *Curator,* "means higher attendance, and higher attendance means better access to government and private funds and grants. The funds allow for better programmes and better museum facilities that attract higher attendance."[4]

BBC Television filming "the world's most expensive picture" at the National Gallery of Scotland.

From the standpoint of museum curators and directors, the message is clear. It doesn't matter how big or small a museum is, it makes sense for it to interest the media in what it's doing.

What kind of Press should museums expect, anyway? What kind of Press, in particular, do museums deserve?

It depends, like many things, on your point of view.

The curator of a well-run museum with modern, attractive displays, changed at frequent intervals and enlivened by the occasional exhibition, might feel that

regular, accurate and supportive pieces in the Press would be a reasonable expectation.

But ask a journalist or a TV news editor how much Press that particular museum – or any other – deserves, and they'd probably say: "None at all, if they don't do anything to justify publicity".

It's the difference between these viewpoints that creates the feeling on the museum side that they don't get as much Press as the collections deserve, and on the side of the media that many museums just don't try hard enough.

*Halliwell's House Museum,
Selkirk. The curator and
his assistants, dressed in a
suggestion of period
costume, brought out the
essence of the occasion...*
The Scotsman
Publications Limited

I talked to news editors, journalists, and other people in television, radio and newspapers to get some idea of what museums are doing to promote themselves in the media. The general impression I got is that museums aren't doing nearly enough.

One senior newspaperman told me that only about half a dozen museums in Scotland keep in touch regularly. He felt that the others could and should be reminding newspapers more often of their existence.

He said museums were just waking up, very slowly, to newspaper requirements. That the situation had been bad, but was getting

better. And that while there were signs of improvement, there was still a long way to go.

So how do we go about improving things?

There are several things we can do that will help.

In trying to improve matters, remember, first of all, to think pictorially.

The power of a photograph can't be overestimated. People may not read every word or even every article in a newspaper, but they glance at every picture. A good picture of one of your exhibits influences the layout of the page on which it appears. You may get twice as many words as would have been the case if the story wasn't illustrated.

And pictures influence people to come and look at originals.

This should be easy, for museums are full of potentially photogenic things. All they need is the right presentation. Simple, graphic examples which focus on the essence of the idea behind the project – and show it in a clear and easily understood way.

Here's an example. The opening of Halliwell's House Museum in Selkirk made the front page of *The Scotsman*. And it was seen on television too.

The centrepiece of the displays was an old ironmongery shop. It had been faithfully reconstructed to look as it did in the days it was open to the public. The essence of the occasion, however, was brought out by the

curator and two of his assistants, dressed in a suggestion of period costume.

It made an attractive picture. It was appropriate. It was eye-catching. Above all, it was simple. When you're thinking of picture ideas, don't make them too complicated. The more easily grasped a visual message is, the stronger the statement it makes.

At the opening of the new Gallery of Modern Art in Edinburgh, a feast of visual material was available both from the permanent collection and the IBM-backed Edinburgh Festival exhibition "Creation". But the photographers preferred a picture of Scottish Secretary of State George Younger flying one of the kites that had been brought in for the opening Gala. The symbolism of celebration was clearly conveyed.

Newspapers and magazines are basically about people. And people are an essential component of any television interview, news item or documentary.

From a Press point of view, an exhibition or display, an historic dress, a suit of armour, a weapon, a piece of furniture or jewellery or a farm implement isn't necessarily interesting in itself. But any object becomes a possible Press picture when it's associated with a person – to humanise it, enliven it, and put it in context – both in scale and in function.

Newspapers have preferences in their choice of the people they photograph. Youth is preferred to age, female to male, children to adults, animals to (but preferably with) people. Indulge Press photographers' foibles, whenever possible. They know, better than you, the kind of pictures most likely to be used in their paper.

Television has particular requirements. Glass showcases present problems because of the reflections, and no matter how well displayed an object may be, it needs to be taken out of the case, or even outside the museum, before meaningful photography can take place.

Don't invite television cameramen to film delicate prints, watercolours or other sensitive objects and then expect them to operate at light levels as low as "50 lux". It can't be done. Radio producers look for a good spokesperson who can conjure up an image by voice alone – voice pictures, in other words.

Search for the human story behind the objects. Who owned them? Who wore them? Who worked with them? Who sailed in them, did battle with them, or played with them? And can any of this be recreated for the cameras?

Museums are in the history business. But history needs to be brought to life if it's to mean anything to the readers, the listeners, and the viewers.

Can a little imaginative showmanship "lift" an exhibit into the orbit the Press inhabit? Two models wearing ringlets were the key to a front page picture which effectively promoted an exhibition of 17th century works by John Michael Wright in the Scottish National Portrait Gallery. The ringlets suggested the period, the models hinted at the subject matter. Again, a very simple idea. But it worked.

The same gallery's very successful exhibition – "Action Portraits" – was launched by the actress Dee Hepburn. We chose her because of her sporting associations in the film "Gregory's Girl" which tied in with the "action portrait" theme. The idea grew naturally out of the subject matter.

Try not to offer television the standard "talking head" interview if there's a chance for more imaginative camerawork. Television is all about movement, which can be something of a challenge with repositories of static objects. A ferocious looking mantrap in a Scottish Museums Council exhibition on poaching was carefully but graphically slammed shut to make a convincing visual point. Henry Moore's "Reclining Figures" on the back of a lorry proved irresistible to Scottish Television when the sculptures were moved to their new home in the Scottish National Gallery of Modern Art.

Competitions, particularly for children, can often generate Press pictures. Children en

Dee Hepburn . . . sporting associations with Gregory's Girl. Scottish Daily Express

César's Compression:
with actress Seretta Wilson.
Scottish Daily Express.
*Junk sculpture lookalike
with scrap metal merchant*
The Scotsman
Publications Limited

masse sell extra copies, and the photo-sales department does business too. Adult competitions are just as effective, as was demonstrated by one to devise a caption for the couple in Roy Lichtenstein's pop art picture "In the car". There were hundreds of entries, and the picture was used repeatedly to illustrate the competition.

Sometimes the price of a new acquisition can project it into the news. In this area, contemporary art galleries have an almost unfair advantage.

The Gallery of Modern Art leapt onto the front pages with the Lichtenstein, whose apparently simplistic comic-strip

appearance prompted headlines like "WOULD YOU PAY £100,000 FOR THIS?"

The same Gallery did it even more spectacularly wih César's "Compression". After several weeks when everything from national television to the *Daily Star* and *Materials Reclamation Weekly* had vied with each other in questioning the use of public funds to acquire what appeared to be a crushed and rusting Renault, a perceptive letter appeared in *The Scotsman*. It read: "Considering the amount of publicity which the National Gallery of Modern Art's new acquisition has had, the £23,000 that it cost has been well spent."

The timing of events can make a crucial difference to their publicity value.

The Scottish National Portrait Gallery commissioned a portrait of The Queen Mother by an Israeli artist. This might have attracted publicity quite successfully on its own account. But when the Trustees of the National Galleries remembered that the Queen Mum's birthday was approaching and cannily timed the launch to coincide, the picture was seen on everything from breakfast television to *News at Ten*.

We can learn a lot from the auctioneers and sales rooms in how to get a visual message across. In miscellaneous collections, there's invariably one object that lends itself to photography when held, worn, or wielded in some way.

In a gallery the paintings have somehow to be made to "come down from the walls" – not necessarily literally. A former Tiller Girl was still agile enough to simulate a high-kick for the photographers in front of Sickert's "High Steppers", and the dancers of Scottish Ballet triumphantly recreated "The Dancing Class" for newspapers and television in the National Gallery of Scotland's major Degas exhibition some time ago. They provided a living, moving tableau – ideal for television.

The Dancing Class *by Degas – recreated by dancers of Scottish Ballet.* Photography by courtesy of The Glasgow Herald.

To get the photographers and the television cameras there in the first place, museums have to remind the Press that they exist. The most common – and the most abused – way of doing this is by means of Press releases.

This isn't the place for me to discuss the fine points of technique when it comes to writing Press releases, so I'll deal with some of the blunt points instead.

The first rule that applies to material sent to the Press is to think of the person at the receiving end.

I spoke recently to some of the people in newspapers, radio stations and television studios who are at the sharp end of our efforts to promote museums.

One thing they all agreed on: there's room for improvement in museum Press releases. Quite apart from the content, it pays to think of the appearance. This is where a splash of colour can help – or a distinctive logo or namestyle.

Here's some of the comments I heard about museum releases: "drab and uninteresting", "dull and dreary-looking", "in need of brightening up" – and all this before anyone had read a word of the content . . .

When it comes to the words, remember that news editors are busy people. They hate Press releases that ramble on in an inconsequential way – so they have to read the whole release to work out if there's anything in it that's worth using or following up. The chances are they won't bother.

Sub-editors hate releases typed in single spacing – which leaves no room for marking-up. And everybody hates releases that have been badly reproduced on a low-grade photocopier.

The secret of writing a usable release is to make the meaning clear in the heading and the first paragraph. This is where you should remember the five "Ws" every young reporter learns about on their first day in the office: Who, What, Where, When and Why.

Who's doing something, what are they doing, where is it happening, when is it taking place, and why?

Newspapers like absolutes: biggest, smallest, longest, furthest, shortest, oldest, youngest, newest. Don't go into vast detail – one page releases are best. Keep the message tight, with short sentences. Avoid academic or museological jargon. And make sure all the facts are checked and correct. Always double-space between the lines, quadruple between the paragraphs. Don't use capital letters, except in the title, never underline anything, and use only one side of the paper. Put a date at the beginning or the end.

Lastly, make sure there's a contact name and telephone numbers which cover not just office hours but evenings and weekends too. Newspapers don't work standard office hours.

When you send out the releases, make sure they're addressed to the right person or department. An envelope addressed to "The Director, BBC" or "The Editor, Glasgow Herald" may arrive too late (if at all) at the point where something might be done about it. Send releases to the News Editor or the appropriate department. In the case of newspapers, if there's a visual angle send a separate release to the Picture Editor. If the item has longer-term, in-depth story potential, send one to the Features Editor as well.

Don't assume a release will be passed around until it reaches someone who's interested in what it's about. Newspaper offices are full of wastepaper baskets, emptied regularly. Most of the contents are Press releases.

Consider the varying needs of the different markets. A local weekly paper might be happy to reprint a five page epic verbatim, but television news editors would greatly prefer a short note drawing attention to the suggested visual content and the possibility of access in advance.

Don't forget the weekly and monthly magazines, some of which have enormous circulations, and all of which have a much longer life than a daily paper or news bulletin. They work to lengthy deadlines, so you should allow three to six months advance notice. The same thing applies to television outside broadcasts. So if you've something spectacular coming up in a few months time, make sure you get a note in to forward planning or future events departments in good time.

The main thing is to communicate – and keep on communicating. To establish, build up and maintain contacts in newspapers, television and radio.

Don't expect instant results.

One radio journalist I spoke to said: "It's just sheer persistence, isn't it? Even if nine times out of ten a release goes in the bucket, something connects sooner or later."

Sometimes impressive results can be obtained by hand-tailoring an idea exclusively to a particular outlet. Exclusives are generally given more space and more thoughtful treatment. But don't, obviously enough, do this with non-repeatable events. Exclusives sometimes fail to see the light of day.

It's a matter of bridging the gap between what the media wants and what you want for your museum. Accept that if you want publicity you have to play the game by the media rules rather than your own. That may sound a bit one-sided, but the truth is that museums and galleries need the media more than they need us.

Time after time, by disregarding basic media requirements, organisations throw away the chance of publicity for important events. I'm talking about Press functions for significant developments or announcements which went largely or completely unrecorded.

What went wrong on those occasions?

Most of them nosedived because the Press were invited on the wrong day of the week, or the wrong time of the day. As simple as that.

Again, I won't go into details of the 101 things that can mar a Press occasion. But let's say just this. If you hold your event in the afternoon, you can wave goodbye to the prospect of television or evening

Louise Nevelson's
Nightscape ... *and seven-
year-old Mandy Haggerty.*
Daily Record

Television crews also like to get film or videotape in the can early so that there's a chance of it making the midday programme (which also helps the chances of it making the early evening news, as it's already edited). Better still, ask television if they'd like earlier access to "pre-shoot": the day before, if it's possible. The later the event is, the bigger the queue to get it edited. Editing facilities are usually limited, and the "hard news" items always get done first. Museums aren't hard news, unless they're on fire.

The choice of day is important, too. Midweek is good, but check the requirements of your local paper. They won't thank you if you hold your "do" on the day they go to press. Saturdays and Sundays are not recommended.

papers. And if you hold it in the early evening, the chance of meaningful Press participation of any kind is very slim indeed.

The best time is between 10 am and 12 noon, which suits most people, and doesn't interfere with anyone's lunch arrangements.

Send the invitations out about a week in advance, and try to follow up with telephone calls the day before.

Mid-morning functions don't suit everyone, of course. No specific time can. The evening papers would prefer something to be set up before 9 am (or the day before). Your local radio station may want to get in a quick interview in time to go out with the lunchtime news.

And if you really want to bury a piece of news without trace, hold it in the early evening on a Friday. That'll almost guarantee it.

So we've looked at the kind of visual ideas that appeal to the Press, ways of improving Press releases, and the best and worst times for Press functions. We're getting nearer a formula for being more "Press-worthy".

It means thinking about publicity at the very start of planning a display or an exhibition.

It means building it into the warp and woof and fabric of our exhibition strategy so we don't put ourselves in the position of having to try and sell the unsaleable, or – just as bad – trying painfully and usually unsuccessfully to graft on publicisable elements at the last minute. And hoping the graft will take.

It means keeping in contact and constantly reminding the Press that we exist: by the flow of Press releases, ideas for photographs, invitations to view new acquisitions and Press functions for important events – with the invaluable added plus of being able to meet and make friends with individual journalists.

It means being responsive to the needs of the media and not putting up barriers when their interest is eventually focussed.

It means striving for total professionalism in our Press relations in matters of punctuality, punctiliousness in returning telephone calls, and accepting that in the interests of publicity, which is worth a lot, that the time of the Press is often more valuable than ours.

In short it means being imaginative and it means being flexible. A sense of humour helps, too. We must never get too solemn, or our museums will be solemn places. Solemnity is not conducive to media coverage.

If all this sounds like uphill, time-consuming work, it needn't be. It's mainly an attitude of mind. It's a bit like a game, in some respects. It's just a question of working out the ground rules.

The best part is that it's a game which everybody can win. The media get the "story", the museum gets the publicity.

The story will never be written or presented in precisely the way a museum would write

or film it or present it, but that isn't important. The important thing is that it's presented in a way the public can understand, and appreciate, and respond to. And they will respond. The result of Press publicity is invariably that more people come through the doors.

This can bring different problems in its wake, of course. Problems of staffing, problems of security, difficulties about ensuring the safety of objects.

But if, as we get more successful at attracting the media, we need to acquire experience in crowd control, so much the better. As the crowds build up, so does our importance in the eyes of the public – and correspondingly of the Press.

For the Press museums get, in the long run, is the Press they deserve. And if we put our minds to it, that can mean – and should mean – more Press and better Press. It's up to us.

Sources

1 *Visitor Attractions Survey,* Scottish Tourist Board, 1983.
2 Richard Grant: "A Survey of Visitors to the Scottish National Museums and Galleries". *Central Research Unit Papers,* Scottish Development Department, June 1981 p. 23.
3 Avril Martin, *Daily Record,* 31 July 1984, p. 19.
4 Susan Lynn Davis, Public Relations – An Imperative in Today's Art Museums, *Curator,* 19 January 1976 p. 63.

John Irving

Peter Maxwell Davies

84

The museum as a cultural centre

Ian McKenzie Smith

Born in Montrose in 1935, Ian McKenzie Smith studied at Gray's School of Art in Aberdeen and then taught in Fife, before being appointed Education Officer with the Council of Industrial Design in 1963. Since 1968 he has been Director of Aberdeen Art Gallery and Museums, while continuing to practise as a visual artist with works in many important collections, and to serve on the boards and committees of many arts organisations.

Art stepped out of the cathedral, art stepped out of the palace, it will step out of the museum if its relevance to society is ignored.

A visit to the museum should be a cultural experience similar to listening to music, reading a book. Objective confrontation with the original object gives the visitor the opportunity of a special kind of experience – an epiphany experience.

The museum has a covenant with its community and can only operate successfully while it sustains the trust and confidence of its community – at all levels – as a home for the Muses – all the Muses. If works of art define our culture – these should be experienced in context and not in isolation.

Most museum programmes can lend themselves to such opportunities and, with a will, exhibitions and related events can help to make sense of the arts in our time.

During a Mobil sponsored exhibition from America the writer John Irving launched his new novel *Hotel Newhampshire* in Scotland.

Peter Maxwell Davies introduced a new film of his work during an exhibition of Orkney photographs.

For a two-year period Archie Hind, the Glasgow novelist, was Aberdeen Art Gallery's writer in residence. Shorter music residencies have been arranged, and the Gallery's studio accommodates artists from abroad for six month periods, resulting in an exhibition within the Gallery and, on occasions, opportunities for local artists to arrange reciprocal residencies.

Aberdeen Art Gallery was the first to accommodate the Scottish Tourist Board's Craftsmen in Residence scheme. Now each summer, visitors have an opportunity to observe a variety of crafts in production while also having the opportunity to see, in

85

Bill Gibb's autumn collection.

context, fine craftsmanship of the past from the collections.

An important showing of Bill Gibb's autumn collection prompted the Friends of Aberdeen Art Gallery to commission a magnificent "Landscape Coat" by his collaborator, Kaffe Fassett. Workshops were conducted for adults and children.

A subsequent gift of a collection of over 3,000 items of costume was directly attributed to the Gallery's commitment to this field.

With the availability of a multi-purpose auditorium within Aberdeen Art Gallery, the promotion of dance performances and participation has been possible. As a major city venue for dance, this art form can be experienced in the context of a major

collection of 20th century painting and sculpture.

Aberdeen Art Gallery's outreach programme has been transformed by the acquisition of a "Travelling Gallery", which in one year has taken a series of topical exhibitions to numerous sites within the city to some 30,000 visitors, many of whom graduate to becoming first time visitors to the Art Gallery.

A properly equipped 'studio workshop' facility allows for many informal and participatory activities especially for the younger visitor.

An intensive programme of such events throughout the year ensures that many develop a healthy attitude of familiarity with their museum.

*Solo dance and
participation*

Travelling Gallery.

Burrell Gallery, Glasgow.

Museums and galleries in Scotland – The future

Allan Stewart MP

John Allan Stewart MP is the Scottish Office
Minister with responsibility for Industry and Education.
From September 1981 until April 1982 he was Minister
for Health and Social Work, and from April 1982 was
Minister for Home Affairs and the Environment.

Mr Stewart first entered Parliament in May 1979,
and is the Conservative Member for Eastwood.

Born on 1 June, 1942, he was educated at Bell Baxter
High School, Cupar, and at St Andrews University,
and Harvard where he was a Rotary International
Foundation Fellow. While at St Andrews University he
was President of the Students Representative Council.

From 1965 until 1970 Mr Stewart lectured in
political economy at St Andrews University.
He joined the CBI in 1971 as Head of Regional
Development and subsequently held the posts of
Deputy Director (Economics) and Scottish Secretary
before becoming Scottish Director in 1978.

Mr Stewart was a member of the Select Committee
on Scottish Affairs until being appointed
Parliamentary Private Secretary to
Hamish Gray, Minister of State
at the Department of Energy in March 1981.

The title I have been given for this talk is a slightly daunting one – "Museums and Galleries in Scotland: The Future". It sounds as if I am being expected to look forward with the aid of second sight or to offer predictions like a writer of science fiction. But I am not sure that my powers stretch that far. Governments may help to shape the future, but they cannot necessarily predict it.

Instead what I would like to do is to offer you some pointers to the sort of future I think Scottish museums and galleries should be aiming for. For a number of reasons, this seems an appropriate time to take stock of the current state of the museums business in Scotland. (And, by the way, I make no apology for using the word "business" in connection with museums, as you will see later.)

Figure from a display on a mediaeval mint, Hunterian Museum, Glasgow.

Working reproduction screw press, Hunterian Museum, Glasgow.

Why is this such a good moment to take stock? Firstly, because there has been such a phenomenal growth in the number and variety of museums in Scotland in recent years. In the last year we have of course seen the opening of two galleries of the front rank in Scotland: the Burrell Gallery in Glasgow and the new National Gallery of Modern Art in Edinburgh. But although they have captured the headlines, we should not forget the many other developments up and down the country, from the splendid Hunterian Art Gallery to the varied smaller museums often displaying some special facet of local history which have sprung up throughout the country. The number of Scottish entrants for the annual Museum of the Year Awards bears witness to the quality of what has been achieved.

But this is also an important moment for reviewing the state of the museums business because it is a time of change at the top, as it were. This autumn we shall be introducing into Parliament a Bill which will establish a new Board of Trustees to run both the Royal Scottish Museum and the National Museum of Antiquities of Scotland which the Secretary of State has already said will form the basis for a new Museum of Scotland. Of course there is a good deal to be done to plan the new museum structure that will take shape when these two national museums come together next year. That is why earlier this year the Secretary of State appointed a special Museums Advisory Board, under the chairmanship of the Marquess of Bute, to consider all aspects of the work of the national museums and to suggest how they should be structured in the future. I know

the Advisory Board is making good progress and I look forward to hearing its recommendations next year, as I am sure you all do. Because of course the work of the national museums affects everyone in the museum profession throughout Scotland in one way or another.

However, the work of the national museums is far from being the whole picture. The local museums have their own traditions and their own needs. In considering what is the best way forward for them a number of different criteria must be applied from those which affect the nationals. In recognition of that we have

Scottish National Gallery of Modern Art, Edinburgh.

Putting finishing touches to a display in About Face *at the Royal Scottish Museum, Edinburgh.*

Bookstall at the Scottish National Gallery of Modern Art, Edinburgh.

asked the Museums and Galleries Commission to undertake a review of the non-national museums in Scotland – something which has not been systematically undertaken for some 20 years. I am pleased to say that the Commission readily accepted this task and the Working Party under the chairmanship of Professor Hamish Miles has already begun its work. It too is hoping to present its report next year.

So there are a number of reasons why this is a particular moment of flux in the history of the Scottish museums movement. What can we expect to achieve from the various studies that are going on? What are the pointers to the future? I should like to suggest one or two which occur to me.

It will surprise no-one if my first point relates to the use of resources. Museums are very often the creation of enthusiasts, people who are prepared to devote a considerable amount of their own time and often their money to see their own particular dream become a reality. That is a wonderful thing for the rest of us, because it means that we get the benefit of their enthusiasm and skills. But what happens when these enthusiasts are no longer around? Someone has to keep the museums running, to make sure that the collections continue to be conserved and properly displayed, that the buildings in which they are housed are properly maintained. All of that costs not a little money. And each new museum that opens stores up those sorts of problems for someone in the future. At the end of the day it is usually local government or even central government which is asked to step in with help, unless a trust has been

established which has been entirely successful in ensuring a constant flow of funds for the maintenance of the museum and its collections.

So my first thought for the future is this. Let us all take a good hard look at each suggestion for a new museum or gallery in whatever capacity it reaches us. Let us ask ourselves not only whether it would be nice to establish, let us say, a collection of street lighting, ancient and modern, in Barrhead, (I don't suggest for a minute that anyone is actually thinking of such a thing), but whether that subject is not adequately covered somewhere else; and even if it is not, whether we really need to preserve such a collection. Funds for museums can be garnered from a wide variety of sources these days – not only from central and local government and the Scottish Museums Council, but from agencies such as the Scottish Tourist Board, the Scottish Development Agency, the Highlands and Islands Development Board, and from private business and industries – but all of this money is finite, and someone has to make the hard choices about how to use it.

I should like to add my voice therefore to those who have suggested that what is needed in the development of museums is a slightly less piecemeal approach than we have now. And this, it seems to me, is essentially a matter in which co-operation between the national museums and the others is necessary. What is needed is something like a national plan for the development of museums in Scotland, although that perhaps suggests a rather more rigid structure than I actually have in mind. I hope that the studies which are

The curator of the Museum
of Flight (an outpost of the
Royal Scottish Museum)
receives the log book of the
last journey of the Vulcan
B2 bomber flown to the
The Scotsman
Publications Limited

currently under way will make a start in setting out the guidelines, but I have no doubt that thereafter it will require continuing co-operation between the Board of Trustees of the national museums on the one hand and the Scottish Museums Council, representing the non-national museums, on the other. I am sure that there will be a continuing rôle here too for the Museums and Galleries Commission. Between them these bodies can ensure that those funding agencies who need advice on how to invest their resources to the maximum benefit of museums and to get the best return in terms of their own remits can obtain it. That way the finite resources at our disposal can be made to go a lot further, to everyone's benefit.

My second message relates directly to the title given to this conference: "Museums are for People". The need for museums to make themselves more attractive both to the expert and to the average man in the street is something which cannot be emphasised too often.

The image of museums in the minds of the public is undoubtedly changing. But there are still plenty of people whose image of a museum is of a sort of tomb, in which items are frozen unchangingly in their cases. You

The Oriental Gallery, Burrell Gallery.

all know that there are fewer and fewer of such museums remaining, but there is still something pejorative in many peoples' minds about the word "museum".

Then too there are many people who, even when they visit the brightest and liveliest modern museum displays, feel that they should not raise their voices. They feel the same inhibitions people feel when visiting a cathedral, or going round a public library. I don't want to suggest that you should all encourage your visitors to shout and scream when they view your exhibits, but is excessive reverence what we really want? And if not, how do you change that? For my own part I would suggest a number of ways in which museums can look to a wider future public than that which they currently enjoy.

The first is to open up museums and galleries more for other activities. I know that there are problems here about the security of items in the collections, and that a number of institutions simply do not have any suitable space in which this could be done. But the potential benefits are obvious, and I am sure that in many instances the difficulties could be readily overcome. The National Galleries in Edinburgh have led the way in recent years by organising a number of concerts on their premises. They have been highly successful. But there is of course no reason why activities should be restricted to those with purely an arts bent. Businesses might welcome the opportunity to hold special receptions or events on museum or gallery premises, and this could help to build up a special relationship from which the institution could well benefit in the future. And there are no doubt other ways of

opening up museums and galleries to a wider public. Indeed, here is an area in which competitions could be run inviting imaginative suggestions from the public as to alternative ways of bringing fresh life into your institutions; there could be a suitable prize, and the chance of putting the best ideas into effect.

The aim should be to make museums more "living" institutions in the future and another way is by the actual involvement of ordinary people almost as living exhibits in themselves. When the Smithsonian Institution brought its splendid exhibition of treasures to the Royal Scottish Museum in Edinburgh last summer I was most impressed by the fact that it brought with it a number of performers to interpret the living American traditions of folksong, jazz and so on. And of course the Japanese regularly grant the appellation of "living treasures" to a number of skilled performers in particular traditional arts. I am not suggesting that we need to go that far, but there is surely more that we can do here to involve living people as an extension as it were of museum collections. This could involve anything from folk-singers and musicians performing music relevant to the collections of a particular museum to skilled workers in the crafts or in different branches of industry displaying techniques which might otherwise be allowed to be forgotten. I know that none of these ideas are new, but there is considerable additional potential waiting to be tapped.

Then too there is the question of how museums are marketed. Clearly there is no point in having a lot of new activities going on in your museum if no-one knows they

Upper Gallery at the Scottish National Gallery of Modern Art.

are happening. It seems an obvious point, yet I know that there is still a feeling in some quarters that it is somehow degrading for a museum to be going out into the market place to attract its customers. All I can say is that that is an attitude that is going to have to be overcome if museums are to face the future positively. Whether we like it or not, all the leisure industries – and here I include museums just as much as, say, football clubs or circuses – are competing in the same market. Whether or not they are charging for admission, they need to attract a wider and more varied public if in turn they are to receive the sort of benefits that can follow – increasing

sponsorship; greater public awareness of their rôle; and better involvement with the people who could become their regular and devoted visitors.

That was what I meant when I referred earlier on to the "museums business". Because museums are as much in business as any company which manufactures its wares or provides a specific service. In a sense museums do both: they manufacture the displays which showcase the items in their care, and they serve the public by interpreting those items to them in such a way as to capture their imaginations and

inform them more thoroughly about what they are seeing.

But like any other business museums and galleries cannot rely on continuing support unless they continue to fill a want. The days when local authorities could altruistically support a museum because their area "ought to have one" without questioning what went into it or how it was run are largely gone. So too, with a few rare exceptions (most of them American!), are the individuals who were prepared to put their hands in their pockets and finance a new museum or gallery without expecting any more in return than their name over the door. If museums are to receive continuing help in the future they must be prepared to learn the rules of business. That need not mean that they should make too many compromises. But they must be prepared to stand in the market place, judge the mood of the crowds and then win the battle for customers by offering them not only something better but something they cannot get elsewhere.

You may wonder why in this brief survey of the future which I see for museums and galleries in Scotland, I have said nothing about the less publicised aspects of their work: the conservation which goes on behind the scenes to prepare items to take their place in the displays which we all admire; the educational work which introduces not only youngsters but many others to aspects of collections which otherwise would be closed to them; the research without which it would be impossible to tell half the fascinating stories surrounding so many of the objects on display. Of course without these services no museum can be really complete. They are the aspects which as often as not ensure the museum its status in the judgment of other museum professionals. But they rarely, if ever, finance themselves. And without the sort of aggressive approach I have been talking about to winning support – both from the general public, from funding sources, public and private, and from the media – museums will simply lose out in the battle to win and retain the aid which they need to keep those essential services going.

I have no doubt that the future for museums and galleries in Scotland is one of great promise. The Scottish Tourist Board recently produced figures which showed that in the course of a year more people visited museums in Scotland than attended football matches. But what those figures don't tell is how often people are coming back to museums. I would be prepared to bet that the vast majority of those museum visitors made one, two or at most three visits to museums in a year.
I would suggest that what we should be aiming to achieve in future is that the majority of people not only go more museums regularly but that they want to keep coming back because, like cinema-goers in the 1920s and 1930s, they cannot afford to miss the next big attraction. I believe that the range and variety of museums and galleries' collections in Scotland is such that, given the right approach, it should not be difficult to build up that kind of enthusiasm in the Scottish public.

Cover photograph courtesy of Scotsman Publications Ltd.

Printed in Scotland for HMSO. Dd 762063/4488 C30 3/85